Live Again

A true story of overcoming loss

By: Tracy Boyd

Influential Productions

Influential Productions

Printing 2009

ISBN: 978-0-9822763-3-4

For Worldwide Distribution
Printed in USA

Pastor Tracy Boyd

About the Author:

Pastor Tracy Boyd is currently co-pastoring at the main campus of Life Christian Church (LCC) in Troy, MI. She and her husband, James, are the proud parents of three beautiful girls. She has spearheaded the development of the worship and arts department, parenting classes, marriage classes, and children's ministries. Along with her mother and two brothers, she co-hosts a TV program called Come Home To Life to bring the message of Christ outside the church walls and into the community. Pastor Tracy is actively involved in the teaching ministry at LCC. She has a way of taking the dynamic truths of the scripture, coupled with her life experience, into a relavent application to everyday life. She is passionate about sharing her methods of success with others, believing that God is not a respecter of persons and can do the same for you.

See more about this author:

tracyboyd.org
or
comehometolife.com

Live Again

A true story of overcoming los

Table of Contents

Live Again

A true story of overcoming los

Foreword

Live Again is an honest story of a young woman whose life is shattered by the loss of her husband and father of her children. It is also a book of how God can and will help you recover beyond your ability to do so on your own. This is a book of God's provision when a person will put their pain into His hand. All of us will one day experience the loss of someone close to us. That is what makes this book such a must read for everyone.

Bishop Keith A. Butler
Word of Faith International Christian Center

Live Again

A true story of overcoming los

Introduction

Once upon a time there was a young girl who truly believed that one day she would be swept off her feet by the man of her dreams. She earnestly prayed that she would know for sure that he was "the one" and that even her family would recognize him and say, "He's the one!" As she came of age to begin courting, there were many who came declaring their devotion to her. She knew in her heart, however, that none of these gentlemen would turn out to be "the one". Then one day she saw a handsome, tall man. There was something about him that kept her attention. Could he be the one? Yes, he is the one! This wonderfully handsome, intelligent, kind man entered her life in a flurry and lovingly swept her off her feet just as she had always dreamed. Their courtship was short, for they knew it was so meant to be. They were married and lived happily ever after. The end.

Isn't that how we all want it to turn out? Don't we love happy endings and hate bad endings? There is something inside of us that yearns for the happily ever after. I believe we yearn for this because in our original creation, we are wired for the happily ever after! We can never be prepared for tragedy, especially a loss. It makes us cringe. But one thing is for sure: we have a loving Heavenly Father who understands the pain and who wants to walk through it with us in a way by which we overcome and actually become stronger.

In 2002, I lost my husband to cancer. He was the man who swept me off my feet, and I truly believed we would live happily ever after. He was 34 years old, I was 35, and we had three beautiful children. I was not prepared. I had no idea it was coming.

If someone had said to me, "Tracy, in August of 2002 you are going to lose the love of your life to cancer and you will be left to raise your three girls by yourself," I never would have believed it for a moment. I would have quoted many promises from God's Word that I have kept close to my heart concerning protection and healing and then said, "Get behind me, Satan!" I have been optimistic my whole Christian life for good reason. God has done tremendous, big, miraculous things throughout my life. He has always been faithful. Diagnosed with an incurable illness in my early teens, I was supernaturally healed. Why? I believe that healing is a part of the salvation that my Creator promised me in His Word. Every limitation that I had experienced in my physical body, including stomach issues, limited vision, a growth on my wrist, and pain in childbirth were all healed over a period of time through applying the Word of God. God had a perfect track record in my life. I found a promise in His Word, applied it to my situation, believed in my heart that He would do it for me, and repeatedly found that His Word works.

Yet, my husband did die. Those who have experienced loss know what I'm talking about when I say, "It's a wound deeper than any physical wound could go. It is a deep, internal pain that is indescribable." Could the God who healed so many limitations in my physical body heal my broken, devastated soul? I was in the middle of the worst fear of my life. Would I ever feel anything again? Would I ever feel safe again?

The answer was YES! God in His great mercy and grace brought me through a healing process that proved again that He is a complete God—healing the spirit, soul and body of man. In the process of my healing there were so many revelations, impartations, and understandings deposited into my soul that brought me healing. I feel so honored to share my journey with you so that you, too, can come to a place of total healing, a place of living again.

Live Again

A true story of overcoming los

Chapter 1: Bitter Endings

"Mrs. Stefano you need to let him go. We need to take him away now." I had been lying in a hospital bed next to my deceased husband for five hours telling him to come back to me. I was unwilling to let go. I needed to hold him...I thought, if they take him away, I can't hold him...I noticed that he was not warm any more.... "Marcus, don't you know I can't live without you?" I overheard the nurses say they had to take "the body" away. I thought, "That's not 'a body.' He is my husband. Can't you understand?" My mom gently took my hand and guided me out of the bed into a separate room. I looked back to see the nurses rolling the bed he was in down another hall, around the corner and he was gone. I was completely numb. The battle was over, and I had lost. I had been in so many hospitals, slept in so many hospital chairs, their beds, and on their floors to be with my husband as we fought cancer. Toward the end, the smells of the hospitals became repulsive. I had seen so much pain and suffering, and now death.

Jesus, I need you. I need you!

While I was aware that something died in me, there was a grace, an enabling power, a presence surrounding me so that I felt as though I was inside a bubble. In this state, I simply did what I was instructed to do. My mom led me through all the paper work. I had no words, no thoughts—only actions.

I can remember the elevator ride down to the parking structure, then sitting in the back seat of some car and simply staring at the seat in front of me, shocked that I had no thoughts—just numbness. Yet the bubble was still there, surrounding me. I wanted the car ride to last, but it didn't. I didn't want to face anything. I wanted to know when I was going to wake up from this horrific nightmare. I wanted to close my eyes and make it all go away.

We arrived late at my house, and my three girls were already sleeping. They actually were all sleeping in my bed, awaiting my arrival. I had been saying for the last month, "Daddy's going to come home soon, and we're going to be a family again." (This last time he had been in the hospital for an entire month.)

What could I say? What should I do? I stared at their beautiful, peaceful, slumbering faces thinking how different those faces would look when I told them the news that they no longer have a father. I felt so desolate for them. How could I make it all better? I recalled when they would fall or scrape themselves and get a "boo boo," and I would say, "Mommy will make it all better," and they had full confidence that I could. This time, I couldn't make it all better. I wasn't ready to wake them out of their sleep to tell them. I lay down next to them and began to caress them gently. All the while, I kept thinking, "What do I do, God? I'm not ready for this! I'm clueless." I began to weep quietly and held on to my kids for dear life.

My mom was so in tune with me (really, so in tune with God) and she knew what to do with me. "Tracy, let them sleep; come to my house tonight and stay with me." There were plenty of family members staying at our house, and Mom lived across the street, so I would still be close to my girls. She guided me out of my bed, and I simply followed.

When I finally laid down, I remember thinking, "How am I ever going to sleep?" I turned on my side and stared at the wall... There it was again: the bubble, the peace, His presence reassuring me that He was with me and reassuring me that the girls and I would be okay. Then my mind drifted to the congregation at our church. "God, what about all the people in the church?" I kept seeing their faces one by one. I pastored with my husband and mother and taught that the same Jesus who healed people in His life and ministry, heals today. He is the same yesterday, today, and forever. I was concerned about how this would impact their walks with God. I cried out, "God, help them. Keep their faith from wavering." I understood in that small moment how Christ's disciples felt when Christ was taken from them to be crucified. In their minds this was not the plan! I'm pretty sure in the heart of Jesus was, "Don't waver, my disciples. You will understand all in due time." I closed my eyes and miraculously fell asleep.

I lie down and sleep; I wake again, because the LORD sustains me. For He grants sleep for those He loves.

—Psalm 3:5, 127:2

Live Agair

A true story of overcoming los

Chapter 2: You Have a Future

Six years have now past since that devastating night. Looking back, I understand why the healing of the soul is such a process. It's because there is such a strong soul tie between us and those we love-especially a husband. It takes time for the soul to adjust to the severing of itself. A husband and wife become one, and Marcus and I were truly one. It took time for my soul to accept that Marcus was no longer here and would never be a part of my life here on earth again. My soul had believed that it was supposed to grow old with Marcus.

It isn't easy to see a future in the midst of that pain while we are experiencing it. We can probably agree that when we have suffered a loss, we find ourselves going through the motions of life as it was before the loss took place. It seems as if every morning is a fight to get out of bed and exist, let alone see a future. Nothing seems to fill the void and there is a sense of discontentment. These feelings are all real. And I felt them all. I knew, however, that God Almighty was bigger than any pain or feeling I was experiencing—that He was the only One who would see me through this difficult time, and that He alone could ultimately heal me. So I clung to God throughout my often painful journey.

The amazing thing about God is that in the midst of our tragedy He is already planning a glorious future! I had just signed the death papers and was entering an elevator when the Lord quietly spoke to my mother. He said to her, "I have a glorious future for Tracy." She needed to hear that I was going to be okay. She was devastated to see me so broken and left with three children to raise without a father. My mother did not tell me at that time that God had spoken to her about my future. I was not ready to hear it. I'm glad she didn't say a word to me, because at that moment, I didn't want a future without Marcus. I didn't. Life couldn't exist outside of Marcus.

God promised us in the passage of Jeremiah 29:11, *"For I know the plans I have for you," declares the LORD, "plans to prosper you and not to harm you, plans to give you hope and a future."*

Amazingly so, God was already past my husband's death and into my future! He did not see my husband as dead, but living in another realm with Him… His concern was for me! Yes, His concern was for me! And God's concern is for you! There is still more life for you; a great future, even though you may not be able to see it now.

It was April 2004, twenty months after Marcus's passing, when I was aware that a miracle had occurred in my soul, and I knew that I was healed. My family (my children, my mom, my brothers and their wives and children) and I were on vacation together at Disney World when all of a sudden I heard God gently say to me, "Your healing is complete." And it was. It wasn't just me who was aware of this healing, but also my family. I have always had the role of "the navigator" in our family. Anytime we travel together, I carry the map. I plan, chart, and lead the way! I generally have opinions and solutions that I am always ready to give, whether or not they want to hear them. For the past 20 months, they had not seen me in any way exhibit those tendencies. I just went along with the program; I really couldn't have cared less what we did, how we did it, or even if we did it. However, while we were in Disney World, I picked up the map and began to chart our course. I looked up to see all of my family members staring at me.

At first I thought I had food on my face or that maybe something was wrong. They finally said, "She's back!" Yes, I was back! Vibrant, full of life, and seeing color again! I had been to Disney a year prior with the girls as an attempt to distract them, and I remember that I was unable to see color. Everything was just blah. Not this time! I looked around and it was beautiful, and I could see color everywhere.

How does this happen within two years? Am I an exception to the rule? Am I special? No! Absolutely NO! God is not partial: He says so![1] What He has done for me, He will do for you. How did I heal? How can you heal? How can you survive? How can you live again? There is a path to healing that I'm excited to share with you. As I share it with you, I believe that you will find healing too.

End Notes:
1. Acts 10:34

Reflect:
We shared in this chapter that it takes time for the soul to heal. Are you ready to go through a healing process?

Act:
God still has a glorious future for you, even though it may not feel like it right now. Read Jeremiah 29:11. Say, "God, I believe You have a great future for me."

Chapter 3: Understanding

We're going to begin our journey of healing with the heading "understanding." When a person experiences a loss or a tragedy, the soul, made up of a person's mind, will and emotions, suffers in health just as a physical body does with disease. Essentially it needs healing. I knew something in me needed to be healed, for there was tremendous pain. Not a physical pain, but a deep internal pain.

Prior to the loss in my life, people would say that I was the kind of person who generally had all the burners on my stove going at the same time, and yet in the initial season of Marcus' passing, just going to the grocery store was a task that seemed impossible. I didn't trust my strength or ability. For the first time in my life I felt so limited. I knew I needed healing.

I was able to begin the process of healing soon after I lost Marcus, because I was taught and understood that my loss was not God's fault, which I will discuss in the next few chapters.   I was familiar with Scriptures that tell us we will encounter the yuck, the negative, the uncomfortable, and at times tragic events, but it is God's job to redeem the unfortunate circumstances, turning them into something incredible that could actually be a blessing for us and others.

Without understanding, we wrestle in our overthinking and trying to find solutions for the tragedy or loss we have experienced. And, many times, we play the blame game, which hinders healing. Have you ever played the blame game? It's in our nature to blame ourselves, doctors, other people, and even God for all the tragedy in our lives. We have squirrelly thoughts and play the blame game because we lack the understanding of who God really is and what truly is going on in this earth! We need understanding.

Understanding Comes by Starting at the Beginning.

To have understanding we have to start at the beginning. Have you ever started a book in the middle and you couldn't figure out what was going on? We have to go to the beginning of a book to really understand what it is about. The same is true when it comes to the workings of humanity and our lives here on earth. Where did pain, suffering and even death come from? We have to go back to the beginning to understand some of the things that are happening right now in our lives.

Our beginning, as a creation, was a perfect world that God made for His crown of creation: mankind. He made man in His own perfect image. In this perfect world, there was no premature death, no divorce, no terminal illness, nor the loss of a dream.

God Wanted a Family

Genesis 1:27 says, *So God created man in His own image; in the image of God He created him; male and female He created them* (NKJV).

Why did God create us? He wanted a family. He wanted children that He could pour His love upon. Why do we have children when we know that they have the potential to give us a bunch of headaches? We want to express our love to them! We can't describe why we love our kids so much. There aren't words to describe our love for them. Even when they're rebellious and unruly, we still love them and would lash out at anyone who tried to harm them. Isn't that true? God wanted a family, and He created humans in His image so He could pour His love out to them. As long as His perfect creation loved, obeyed and simply trusted Him, the perfect world continued.

Mankind Chose Another

Mankind, out of his own free will, chose another world. In the original perfect world that God had created, a crafty being entered, deceived and persuaded God's magnificent creation that another world, a better world, existed. In this new world, the crafty being convinced God's children that they no longer would have to love and trust their Creator, but rather they would be their own rulers, that they could do what they wanted to do, at any time they wanted. This crafty being offered them self-rule, or independence, from God. They were told that they no longer would have to be ruled by anyone. They listened to and believed that lie.1 It is a lie that people are still struggling with today.

Why do we give our children boundaries and want them to trust and obey us? We know that if they follow the boundaries we have set for them, truly trusting and obeying us, they will be safe and have a good future. We as parents know what is out there-the good, the bad, and the ugly—so we want to steer our children to success. Boundaries are for their blessings. God said the same thing: "Just love and obey Me; trust Me and this perfect world that I have created for you will continue."

We don't like for people to tell us what to do! I had a conversation with one of my teenage children recently. She was struggling with an instruction I had given her, and I said, "I know what you're thinking, 'When I get older, I'm just going to do what I want to do.'" She said, "How did you know?" I told her that I did the same thing at her age! The desire for self-rule, thinking we know a better way to do things, is in all of us!

Plan B

The perfect world that God created ended because sin entered into the world making it imperfect. Year after year the effects of sin became more evident: sickness, disease, poverty, plagues, disasters, strife, jealousy, and greed are just a few. We can see thousands of years later that the effects of sin are still present and getting worse. We are not living in the God-created, perfect world.

As any loving parent would, God had a Plan B, because the first plan did not end in "happily ever after." I can't watch a movie that doesn't end happily. I have a problem with it. When anyone invites me to watch a movie, I'll ask, "Does it end well?" If it doesn't, I can't watch it. I get too involved with it. We're not the only ones who want to live happily ever after. God wants it for us too. It is actually His idea, not ours.

The best way to describe Plan B (or even Plan C, D, E and so on) is by way of a GPS system. When you have a GPS system, you enter the address of the location where you want to go, and it gives the shortest path to follow in order to reach your destination. How many of us have decided not to follow the plan we are given and have made a left instead of a right? Does the GPS lady berate us, "I can't believe you missed it! Are you stupid?" NO! What's great about the GPS is if we choose to go in a different direction, it recalculates a new route and still directs us to our destination. We can choose so many lefts instead of rights, but it will continue to adjust and direct us where we need to go. That's God. He will adjust and try to get us back on a path of success, to a path of wholeness. It may take us longer to get there when we insist on going our own way, ignoring His directions, but He still always directs us to wholeness.

So God enacted Plan B. He sent His Son in the likeness of man to take away the sin nature that was passed down to every man. On the cross Jesus bore the sin of mankind and made a way for a perfect God to, once again, have oneness with His creation. When someone becomes a Christ follower, God's Spirit comes into that person, changing his very spirit to be like his Father, like God. Again, we were created in God's image, so when we receive Christ, we are reunited with that image. We are just like Him in our spirit.

Plan B was to reunite us to the original position which was lost in that perfect garden. When you are born anew, the potential is released immediately on the inside of you to navigate through a negative world.

With plan B, although the heart is changed to be like God, the world is still influenced by sin. Sin is still in the earth and the earth is still influenced by a crafty imperfect being, the devil. This may be new to you, this idea that the devil exists. You may laugh at the statement that the devil is real, because you think he's just a guy in a red suit with horns and a pitchfork, but he is real. In order to understand God and His plan for wholeness in your life, you need to know that there is indeed a god (small g) of this earth and his name is Satan, and that it is he who is doling out all the bad junk in this world. God is only doling out the good. While Jesus was on the earth, He made mention of Satan being the "god of this earth."2

Jesus Uncovered the Workings of the Devil

When Jesus was on the earth He took great pains to uncover the workings of this crafty being, the devil. Jesus said in John 10:10, *"The thief comes only to steal and kill and destroy; I have come that they may have life, and have it to the full."*

Now notice this. This is Jesus speaking: He said, "Guys, guess what? There's a thief, he's called the devil. He's been around forever, and he comes to bring destruction, to steal, kill and destroy. But guess what, guys? I came to give life! I came to give you a way through! I came to give you a life that's full!" Jesus said that!

First Peter 5:8-9 NIV says, *"Be self-controlled and alert. Your enemy the devil prowls around like a roaring lion looking for someone to devour. Resist him, standing firm in the faith..."*

Interesting how it says that the devil is looking for someone to give him a way in so that he can destroy. The most common way is by our ignorance of his dealings. Jesus said RESIST him! If He tells us to resist him, it means that we can. It means that Jesus has placed something in us that has the power to resist the devil—to resist his destructive stuff.

Here's one more. Jesus said this in John 16:33, *"I have told you these things, so that in Me you may have peace.*

In this world you will have trouble. " In other words, He says that tragedies and storms will come your way, but then He says, *"But take heart! I have overcome the world."*

Therefore, if we're connected with Him, although trouble may come and the adversary may send things our way, God, our Father said, "Take courage, for if you're connected to Me, we'll walk through it together and overcome." We're victors!

We are Still Living in a Fallen World

My main point here in regard to understanding is this: we're still living in a fallen world, with negative forces constantly pushing against anything that's good. If something is good, there seems to always be a negative force coming against it. The devil is the god of this negative force, and is at work trying to destroy our lives. People have often asked why the devil wants to mess with us, and I say, "If you want to get to me, mess with one of my kids." Isn't that true? Every time the devil messes with us, he's getting to God because we are His creation, we're His kids. The devil cannot stand that we are made in God's image and have the potential to have Christ live on the inside of us. He hates it. So, he's out to destroy lives. I'm not going to go any further with that, because that is another book in itself. The understanding we need, in going forward in our healing process, is that the roots of the bad things that happen to us are a result of a fallen world that is manipulated by a crazy being. The only hope of having a healed, whole, full life is through Christ.

Live Again

A true story of overcoming los

End Notes
1. Genesis 3
2. John 14:30

Questions for Chapter 3:
1. We mentioned in chapter 3 that we live in a fallen world. What does that mean?

2. When one is born anew (receives Christ), what gets changed and reunited to God? What are the results?

3. Why does the devil mess with humanity?

Reflect:
Although you are going through a loss, God longs to navigate you through to healing and wholeness—turn to Him! If you haven't received Christ as your personal Lord and Savior, ask Him into your heart right now. It is the only way of getting your spirit healed and in one accord with God.

Pray this prayer:
"Jesus, I want to be born anew. I receive You into my heart. Be my Lord and Savior. Forgive me of all my sin. Help me to live with and for You."

Act:
Say Psalm 37:23 (NKJV) "Father, in Jesus' name, I believe You are ordering my steps toward the healing of my soul."

Study question answers found on pages 184-190

Live Again

A true story of overcoming los

Chapter 4: Choices Shape our Lives

As we mentioned in the previous chapter, most people are completely unaware that there is a negative force pressing against anything that is good in their lives. This negative force manipulates our choices. Every day we make choices that cumulatively make up who we are and what we get out of life. No one forces us to make those choices. We choose how hard we're going to work, we choose the college we want to attend, we choose the occupation we want to pursue, who we're going to marry, who we're going to be intimate with, what we'll eat, where we'll live. We choose.

Deuteronomy 30:19-20 says, *This day I call heaven and earth as witnesses against you, that I have set before you life and death, blessings and curses. Now choose life, so that you and your children may live and that you may love the LORD your God, listen to his voice, and hold fast to him. For the LORD is your life, and he will give you many years.*

Our Environment Shapes our Choices

Most of us would say, "I'm going to choose life! I'm going to choose blessing!" We can all agree. However, this is the problem: all of our choices are influenced by the environments in which we now live or the environment in which we've been raised. Our environments, which are basically made up of our observations, our associations and our teachings (OATs)[1], have all shaped who we are and have influenced us in how we choose the things that we choose. Our will has been shaped by our environment. Let me give you a couple of examples:

My mom was raised in an environment where education was not a big deal. She was raised in a small town in Italy. After she got married, she came to America. God, by His providence, brought her here, and I'm so grateful. She moved from one environment, a little town in Italy, to a larger town, here in America. She was in a new environment with different kinds of people, new observations, new teachings, new associations, and all of a sudden, education was important! As a result of her new environment, she began to influence us to obtain higher education. Had she stayed in her original environment, she probably wouldn't have influenced us to pursue higher education because where she was raised, education wasn't a big deal. Her environment influenced her choices.

She took the new values as her own and created an environment in our home by talking education, education, education. We were also surrounded by new associations (friends and neighbors) who spoke of going to college as well, as if it were the only acceptable reality. It's just what everyone did. We had heard the reasons, so we understood why people went to college, but when it came to our flesh, we really didn't want to go because it's work. But we were urged to go, so that we could improve our lives, and we heard it, and we heard it, and we heard it: "You're going to have a better life! You're going to get a better job! You need to go to college!" We were influenced by that environment, and low and behold, we all went to college.

Another example of how strongly our environment

shapes our lives is seen frequently through my occupation. A young lady is raised in a home where her mother,
sister, and aunt all had babies out of wedlock, and they
are all on welfare and barely getting by. The probability
of that young lady not doing what she has seen is very
slim. That environment (her OATs) will typically cause
her to make the same choices that were made by those
around her.

Very few choose another direction than the one that
they're raised in. My new husband is one of those few.
He was raised in a home that is different than the one
he is in today. He came from a safe, comfortable, and
caring home, but the mentality was not one of ambition, and the family struggled financially. As a result,
he chose to leave that environment at a young age and
placed himself in a completely different environment.
It was hard—even grueling at times. To make a long
story short, he rose in corporate America and was doing remarkable things in the automotive industry. He
made a decision that if he was going to go anywhere in
life, he needed to change his environment, his observations, associations and teachings, so that his mind
could be exposed and enlightened to more opportunity,
and thereby be influenced to make other choices.

God Understands...His Grace is Available

God understands the environments that we have been
raised in are not necessarily the ones we may have chosen. In His grace, in His wonderful grace, He sends people across our paths to encourage us to accept His Son
and choose a new environment (with new OATs). I call
it (this new environment) the body of Christ, a church
filled with great teachers and mentors who can begin to
help us see God's Word. God's Word is His perfect will

for our lives. It helps us live a wildly successful life and take on a new mentality that will influence our choices to be positive. We have so much negative coming at us, we need to be in an environment that's positive so that we can make wise choices.

I can use my family as an example. Prior to our becoming Christ followers, our house was very volatile. As full-blooded Italians, we were loud, obnoxious and I need to emphasize, volatile. My parents were not happily married so there was a lot of conflict and stress. When my mom was pushed to the end of her anger stick, food would start being thrown around. This included anything she could get her hands on: watermelon, steaks, peppers, et cetera! The point is that it was a volatile home and the environment caused me to have issues with my digestion. I had low self-esteem, insecurity and fear. I was riddled with fear on the inside. There were certain foods I couldn't eat; it was ridiculous. I had to develop a routine to make myself fall asleep.

Obviously our environment was far from being whole. In the middle of our chaotic mess, my mom became a Christ follower through a wonderful experience, and shortly thereafter, I did as well. This new and indescribable peace entered our home! I began attending a church that equipped me to overcome negative things. Not just to cope with them, but really overcome them. I was taught how to deal with life issues through a life manual called the Bible. I learned that the Bible was God speaking to me about how to live my life.

Think about this: when you purchase a piece of equipment it usually comes with a manual. If you're like me, you will read it and you'll put that piece of equipment together the way the manual says because you don't want extra parts leftover, right? Whether you use it or not, everyone understands the purpose of the manual and understands that if we follow the manual then we'll get the most out of that piece of equipment. God has left us a manual as well. If we follow it, we can have a wildly successful life.

The point is, I was living in one environment, and miraculously I entered a new environment. I didn't leave my home, but now my new observations, associations, and teachings began to re-shape me to think positively—to think as my Father in heaven thinks...to think in line with the Word of God. It taught me how to overcome conflict, how to deal with strife and fear. I was learning all of these things and began to put them to practice. My mentality was being completely changed by these wonderful teachings. My choices were influenced by my new environment. Had I stayed in the old environment, my life would have been completely different than it is today. Because, again, our environment shapes the choices that we make.

We have Chosen the Positive and Negative Things in our Lives

Believe it or not, we have chosen the positive and the negative things in our lives (though we hate to hear it. Again, our choices are influenced by our environment. I don't think that we're even aware that we're making choices all of the time. It just happens. We get to a point, and then all of the sudden we're saying, "How did I get here?" Have you ever said that? The truth is that we've allowed it in some way (ouch). I'll take it even further. We choose the foods that we eat. Whatever we choose to put in our mouths goes in; whole grains, vegetables, lean proteins don't just fly in our mouths. We have to put them in.   God will let you eat as much chocolate cake as you want.   He won't stop you, will He?   (Did you ever try it?)

Let's say a person has seen his doctor and his doctor has basically informed him that he needs to stay away from certain foods because, for some reason, the way his body is made up, he's not processing those foods appropriately and so they can bring him much harm. This person says, "I don't want to; I'm going to eat as much chocolate cake as I want," and he does!   Let's say he dies prematurely.   My question is this: was it his time or was it his choice?

Let's say there is really bad weather outside.   There is a maverick who loves to fly planes and he needs to get to another city.   He is told he shouldn't fly because there is very bad weather and it is extremely dangerous to fly. He says "Aw shucks, I'm going to fly in that weather, and I'm going to be just fine!   That warning is for people who don't know what they're doing."   This guy takes off in the plane, and in a short time, the plane crashes and he dies prematurely. I ask you again, was it his time or was it his choice?

We also choose how much stress we want to build into our lives by how we live our lives and specifically by how we think. Science and doctors have proven that stress brings on many of the diseases that we have today. Stress is a result of our thoughts, or our interpretation of situations.   Our thoughts are shaped by our environments (OATs).   Research shows that approximately 87 percent of sicknesses are directly related to our thought life.[2]

Today so many people have a hard time dealing with

stress because they haven't been taught how to manage their thoughts when stress hits. They haven't been in an environment that gives them tools for overcoming stress. And it doesn't help people deal with overcoming stress, when stress, in general, is so accepted. Many believe there is no way to escape stress, that it is just a part of our lives. Some people believe that stress is an indicator that they are working enough, and it has become their security blanket. They can't imagine living without it.

In general people don't understand that stress is a result of their mind interpreting their situation. When a person chooses to keep unforgiveness or bitterness in their heart toward another person who may or may not have actually done something wrong to them, it creates immense stress in their body. When they choose to keep it, seething in it, and it stays in there a long time, it has been proven by medical studies that stress can destroy the inside of a body. Have you ever met a really bitter person? It's likely they're not going to live long. Stress eats them up on the inside.

Proverbs 14:30 says, *"A heart at peace gives life to the body, but envy rots the bones."* Negative thoughts and emotions such as envy, bitterness, and unforgiveness have a negative or adverse effect, somehow, on our bones. Now in the center of the bone is a thicker liquid substance called marrow. I'm not a doctor, but I can summarize it by saying that when our immune system, which is all that blood-flowing stuff, is compromised, that marrow begins to dry up. Stress compromises an immune system. When the immune system is compromised, the organs begin to malfunction. So let me ask you a question: if a person chooses to continue in emotional turmoil, refusing to get free, refusing to go to somebody and say, "I forgive you," and decides to hang on to it, thinking he has a right to do so (and he may very well have a real reason such as abuse or being taken advantage of), will their body break down? Absolutely! The unforgiveness and bitterness is not hurting anyone except the person who holds those feelings close to their heart.

A friend of mine uses the example that holding un-forgiveness against someone is like drinking poison and hoping that the other person will die. It's just not going to happen. If you're drinking poison, you will die, not the other person who offended you. Forgiving is for our benefit. It heals us more than it heals the person who has hurt us! Although we have a free will to keep the negative emotion, it has the potential to kill us. Is it worth dying over?

Suppose a person says, "I can't forgive; I can't let go." If he dies prematurely, was it his time or was it his choice?

I remember my mom telling me about an incident where a friend of hers was dying of a sickness. As my mom was praying for her, she heard from the Lord that her friend had unforgiveness against her previous pastor. My mom immediately went and shared with her what she had heard from the Lord. Her friend said it was true, but that she was unable to forgive her previous pastor. She died shortly thereafter.

What if people choose to be sexually promiscuous and they contract a sexually transmitted disease and die prematurely? This is happening all the time! Was it their time to die or was it their choice that brought on death?

We are hearing more and more information about how our diet, exercise, drinking water and decreasing our stress levels affect our longevity. How many are really taking that seriously and choosing to do something in moderation with the above? Choices are powerful. They shape our destiny and are influenced by the environment that we allow ourselves to be in.

It is profound to think that God is limited to the boundaries of our choices. Think about it. Our awesome Creator gave us a free will. I'm pretty sure that when Adam was about to take that fruit and eat it, God was saying, "No, no, no, no, no, don't, don't, don't!" Doesn't every parent want to do that? But we have to let our children make their own choices. God gave us a free will. He didn't want robots; He wanted children who love Him out of their own free will! I'm fully convinced that God tries to spare us of wrong choices, but we have a hard time hearing and really obeying Him.

Ezekiel 18:30-32 says, *"Therefore, O house of Israel, I will judge you, each one according to his ways, declares the Sovereign LORD. Repent! Turn away from all your offenses; then sin will not be your downfall."*
(In other words, "Come on, make some right choices, make some right choices.")

"Rid yourselves of all the offenses you have committed, and get a new heart and a new spirit. Why will you die,, O house of Israel? For I take no pleasure in the death of anyone, declares the Sovereign LORD. Repent and live!"
Choose.

Do you see those choices that we have? Again, in our natural minds we would never want to choose something that is harmful to us. It's our environments (our

OATs) that shape our thinking, and our thinking shapes our choices.

End notes
1. Spoken by Kenneth Hagin Sr. during a message given

2. Who Switched Off My Brain, Dr. Caroline Leaf, 2007 switch on your Brain PTY Ltd. Pg. 4

Questions for Chapter 4:
1. What influences our choices?

2. For the most part, have we chosen the life we currently have?

3. According to Proverbs 14:30 what can eat us up on the inside, affecting our immune system?

Reflect:
Who in my life is heading me in a positive direction, and who is leading me into a negative direction? With whom could I spend more time, and with whom could I spend less time?

Act:
Create a new boundary for yourself. Purpose to put yourself in a healing environment this week.

Study question answers found on pages 184-190

Live Again

A true story of overcoming los

Chapter 5: Don't Play the Blame Game

Foundational Principles for My Healing

My understanding regarding my environments (observations, associations and teachings) shaping my thinking and directing my choices, led me to foundational
principles that brought me healing or allowed me to go
on a path of healing with God. I had a clear understanding that tragedies, troubles, storms and loss that come
into our lives are a result of the following:

1. A fallen world that is flawed—where negativity is
pressing against anything that is good

2. Choices that we've made

3. Choices made by those who love us or those who are
in our lives

> Recently I talked to a lady whose fiancé made an
> unwise business deal. Even though she warned
> him and told him not to, he chose to do it. The
> business decision involved her money as well as
> his. They both went bankrupt. His choice affected
> her.

4. Demonic influences:

> Ephesians 6:12 NIV says, *For our struggle is not
> against flesh and blood, but against the rulers,*

against the authorities, against the powers of this dark world and against the spiritual forces of evil in the heavenly realms.

We can't see the "powers of this dark world." They are angelic beings that wreak havoc on people's lives. When we walk in ignorance with the above we are taken advantage of!

I said all that I said, right here, for this reason: it's about the blame game. Generally when a loss happens, the first thing many of us do is blame God. Don't we? I've heard this, "Well, God must have allowed it. He must have had a reason." It seems that when we say this, it's as if there's this nebulous unseen thing out there and no one can figure out why this stuff happens. I believe that in some cases there are mysteries that only belong to God. Many times, however, this stuff happens because of the choices that we've made. So we go into the "why God?" mode and get angry, asking ourselves, "Why did this happen to me?"

We want to recognize the four things that bring loss (a fallen world, choices that we've made, choices made by those who love us or those who are in our lives, and demonic influences) because if we blame God, how can we run to Him for healing? God is the only One who can heal a soul. No counselor can do that. It's hidden—it's so deep inside of us. But if we blame God, we can't run to Him. So let's not blame God.

Blaming Ourselves

On the other side of blaming God, there is another ditch we can fall into: we blame ourselves. During that first week after Marcus had passed, I was struggling with all kinds of wild thoughts, blaming myself for his death. Maybe I didn't pray enough, say the right things, or make the right choices. Maybe if I had seen that doctor instead of this one...tried that treatment... maybe, maybe, maybe. I was riddled with guilt. Has anybody done that? That particular week, I was scheduled to meet with my spiritual father, Bishop Keith Butler. He had done Marcus' home-going service and took me under his wing to walk through the difficult season. No one knew that I was struggling with guilt and blaming myself. I didn't tell my own mother. I was aware that I was being "played" as a puppet. I arrived at Bishop's office, walked in and found him sitting behind his desk. I hadn't even greeted him, when all of a sudden he stood up with fire in his eyes, pointed his finger at me and said, "It's not your fault!" The weight of the world lifted from me with just those words. Oh, the love and mercy of God! Bishop began to share things about the issues that were at hand. What he said brought such healing. That one conversation allowed me to continue in the healing process. I am so thankful for the body of Christ. I am so grateful for people who are sensitive to God, who can give us an encouraging word.

The Struggle with Premature Death

Our natural minds struggle with premature death because it's unnatural. We resist it on the inside. It's not supposed to happen. As a person who we love ages, there's a natural preparation that comes as they become more limited in what they can do. Think about a woman who is pregnant. What would happen if she woke up nine months pregnant? She couldn't sustain it. She needs the slow, gradual growth to adjust physically and emotionally, to prepare for what is coming.

Somehow we can naturally adjust to things over a period of time. As those whom we love become more limited, not thinking straight, incapacitated, et cetera, our souls begin preparing for something that's coming. When they pass at an old age, we're actually happy because we know they've gone to be with the Lord and they are free to live again in Heaven, without any limitations. We saw that, although they were here, they were no longer living freely here—they could no longer give us the wisdom we were accustomed to. They couldn't give us the comfort they used to give us. We accept that it is time.

It is still very hard, especially for an older couple, if they've been with a person for thirty-five plus years and then one passes. In these cases, often times the spouse who is left no longer wants to live and wonders why he is still here on earth. He misses his "other half" desperately. It's amazing how, with elderly couples who have been together for a long time, the surviving spouse passes soon after the passing of his/her spouse. Without that person, he loses the desire to live. He doesn't know how to exist without the other. Healing is so necessary. The grace of God is available and must be received. Premature death, however, seems so unnatural, and so we resist it.

The best way for a person to leave this earth is that the body gives up at a ripe old age. There are many examples in the Word of God of people who were very old and knew their time was approaching to leave the earth. They would gather their family together, assigning responsibilities and blessings. In essence, they put their house in order. Once they were finished, they would say their last goodbye, lie down and simply fall asleep. That's the best way to go.

It doesn't make a person bad, or less of a person, because he died prematurely or died of an illness. I don't want us to go there. We can't comprehend the cumulative choices or the environments that shaped that person. We don't understand the demonic forces that came against him. I don't even want to go there! It's none of my business!

Marcus was a wonderful person! He was so funny, handsome, compassionate, kind, and simply a terrific individual! He passed prematurely when he was thirty-four years old. Did it make him a bad person or less of a person? No, not at all! There were issues, ghosts that he dealt with. There were abuses in his past and maybe he didn't know how to deal with them. I don't know. A couple of days before he passed, I remember walking into his hospital room and these words rose right out of me, "Marcus, you're forgiven." I had no idea I was going to say that. I knew it was the Spirit of God speaking through me to him. Marcus looked at me as if he had never heard those words before. I knew we were in trouble. Maybe he felt unworthy of the grace of God. I don't know. I do believe that when he left his cancer—ridden body and experienced true freedom, he probably said, "I am never going back into that body again. I don't care how much you're screaming for me, Tracy. Never!" He experienced emotional and physical freedom that he had never experienced before in his life. We're left with the loss. We're left with the pain. He's having a blast!

God's Design is Long Life

I didn't think it was Marcus' time to go. I was aware of so many wonderful truths regarding long life that allowed me to run to God and not blame Him. God's Word, and even science, proves that God's perfect desire is for us to live a full life. Psalm 91 reflects on our rights and privileges as Christ-followers to be protected and to live a long life.

Psalm 91:14-16 says, *"Because he loves me,"* says the LORD, *"I will rescue him; I will protect him, for he acknowledges my name. He will call upon me, and I will answer him; I will be with him in trouble, I will deliver him and honor him. With long life will I satisfy him and show him my salvation."*

Long life, that's God's best.

Here are some more Scriptures:
Genesis 6:3 says, *Then the LORD said, "My Spirit will not contend with man forever, for he is mortal; his days will be a hundred and twenty years."*
Psalm 90:10 says, *The length of our days is seventy years — or eighty, if we have the strength; yet their span is but trouble and sorrow, for they quickly pass, and we fly away.*

We can see from these Scriptures that it is His will for our lives to be long. If a person lives to be eighty or ninety, we often say, "Oh they lived a full life," right? It seems that science is beginning to prove what the Bible says about our life-span. I recently read about gerontology—the science that studies how we age. Scientists who study cell regeneration estimate the human cells can successfully divide 50 times. When you do the math, that makes a lifespan out to be 115-120 years!

Researchers are still baffled as to what is the force behind all this.1

The Bible is clear that God's best is for us to experience long life, and science even backs it up. Again, there are reasons why one dies prematurely. This topic interested me so much that I spent six months studying and teaching a class called "Road Blocks to Healing."

Accept a New Life

We can't blame God. We can't blame ourselves. We have to accept a new life without the person we've lost. This is a hard one! We have an aversion to that. We have an aversion to going on without them, because we truly believe no one can do what they did for us or fill what they filled in us. Nobody can give the peace, wisdom and comfort they gave us. God understands. It is absolutely true, no one can fill the spot of that person, but God can heal that spot and open us back up for someone else to fill again. We don't feel safe or secure. We can't perceive wholeness outside of the loss. God wants to fill that place, to heal that place. He wants to adjust the GPS system with a new plan. We have to allow Him to do just that. As a Christ follower, God wants to take us through a healing process and begin shaping our new future. However, we have to choose healing.

Isaiah 43:2-3 presents a wonderful promise that I've often thought about:
When you pass through the waters, I will be with you; and when you pass through the rivers, they will not sweep over you. When you walk through the fire, you will not be burned; the flames will not set you ablaze.

For I am the LORD, your God, the Holy One of Israel, your Savior.

He didn't say that we wouldn't go through it. He said that we would avoid some troubled waters. You may go through some fires, but God's going to be with you. He's going to carry you through. Here is an example to illustrate this wonderful promise: Let's say there's a blazing forest around me. I'm holding one of my children, who happens to be a toddler, and I know the way out of the forest. I'm making my way through the forest with my child totally covered and close to me. My child is not concerned about one thing, because she knows I'm going to get her to safety. That's how it is with us and God. He wants to carry us to safety, to get us to the other side of wholeness, to an overcoming life. I'll say it again, John 16:33 says, *"I have told you these things, so that in me you may have peace. In this world you will have trouble. But take heart! I have overcome the world."*

He never said that we would avoid trouble. He never said that. Trouble is in the world! The minute you walk out your door, there's trouble. He wants to navigate a path through those rough waters to get you through to the other side of wholeness, living again by His power and strength. A part of that path is hearing His voice.

Hearing His Voice

Years ago, I learned in a church that I was attending (it was very similar to the church I attend now!) that I could hear God's voice. Wow! Me? I can hear God's voice? I thought only special people, like those spiritual people who stay home all day to pray, hear God's voice..

I learned that I'm His kid and He wants to talk to me just as I talk to my mom. The primary way He trained me, and He trains all of us to hear His voice is through the Bible, His Word. The Bible is His voice to us. But many times we're not used to His voice, and the Bible seems very hard to understand. So sometimes we need people to help us understand.

I needed people to help me understand. We can compare this to a baby coming into the world. A baby doesn't know the language of the home. But by being in that environment, he begins to understand the language. He also becomes very sensitive and can distinguish mom's voice from everybody else's voice. I can say, "Taressa!" and my daughter looks up. And when my children call me, "Mom!" it doesn't matter who is in the room, or how many voices are around, I hear that "Mom!" being called. I can hear it. I can distinguish that voice. Children are trained to our language, to our voice, and it's the same way that we have to train our ear to be sensitive to God's voice by being in the Word of God.

Years ago I developed a habit of talking with Jesus every day. I had no idea that I was training my ear to be sensitive. The reason I started reading the Bible and even talking to Jesus is because I used to watch my mom go and talk to God and read her Bible. All these powerful, miraculous things were happening in her life. I thought, "Well, she goes in that room and she talks with Jesus and reads that Bible, so I'm just going to do what she's doing. I'm going to get those powerful things happening in my life!" Low and behold I was being trained to hear His voice. It is the greatest thing that any of us should ever strive for. It will prevent much heartache in our lives.

In the difficult seasons in my life, when I had a hard time hearing for myself because of the stress and the pain, members of my church and my family helped me to hear His voice. They helped to navigate me through those difficult times. I encourage you to get in an environment that can teach you the Word of God in a practical way so that you can begin to change some environments that you are currently in. It will spare you much and strengthen you greatly.

The Bible says in Matthew 7:24-25, *"Therefore everyone who hears these words of mine and puts them into practice is like a wise man who built his house on the rock. The rain came down, the streams rose, and the winds blew and beat against that house; yet it did not fall, because it had its foundation on the rock."*

I know that winds, storms—you name it—beat against my life in that season, but they didn't destroy me because of my foundation in Christ. My healing was founded on Jesus Christ. And that Scripture continues to say, *"But everyone who hears these words of mine and does not put them into practice is like a foolish man who built his house on sand. The rain came down, the streams rose, and the winds blew and beat against that house, and it fell with a great crash."*

So this says to me that the winds, the storms, the junk, are going to come against everybody. Everybody! It's a product of life, right? But through Christ we can weather them. We can navigate through them. We can be stronger, be better people, and have great futures despite the storms.

I avoided many accidents and trouble because I was in

a place of hearing. I can give you testimony after testimony. One time my family was just about to go out the door when I got a call from mom, "Hey! You know I was praying ... just keep your eye on Daniela. There's something going on. Just watch her. There's some kind of danger." We were alerted. We went on with our plans, which involved going swimming. However, I was very alert. I was watching, keeping my eye out to recognize if there was something planned against her. I remember I turned for one instant to get her swimmies and in that instant she walked into the pool. Because we were warned, we remained sensitive and aware and so we saw it immediately. We jumped in the pool and scooped her up. She was holding her breath! Nothing had happened to her. If we are listening, God will forewarn when there are some things coming our way. It's profitable to learn to hear His voice.

Stay Connected

When we are weak, it's imperative to be around those who are stronger, who know how to use tools to help us. Let me ask you a question. Let's just say you're in a jungle in a foreign country, and we're at war with that country. You have to get through that jungle and there's a machine gun on the ground and you're surrounded by enemies. Whom would you choose to navigate you through the jungle, a military officer or a culinary artist? It's imperative that we surround ourselves with strong people to help us when we're weak. In my weakest moments, I knew there were people praying for me. There were times as I walked through my house that I would have this full awareness that at that particular moment someone was praying for me. I could sense my loving heavenly Father saying, "You're not by yourself, Tracy."

I've got you covered."

God is aware of your pain. He wants to heal you. He wants you to live again. He has a great future for you. For healing and restoration, run to God! Don't blame Him... You need Him!

End notes:
1. Cherry, Reginald. The Bible Cure. Orlando: Creation House, 1998- Page 8.

Questions for Chapter 5:
1. What were the foundational principles that allowed me to heal...to run to God?

2. Have you found yourself blaming God? What does this prevent us from getting?

Reflect:
Have you been struggling with guilt? Have you been playing the blame game; blaming God, others or yourself for all the tragedy in your life? Stop! The blame game does not lead to healing. It's not worth it! Look again at the foundational principles to help you put the blame in the right place.

Act:
When blaming thoughts rise up, say, "I refuse to place blame in the wrong place. Help me God to run to You."

Begin seeking to hear God's voice. Say, "According to John 10:4-5, I hear God's voice and I will not follow the voice of a stranger. You, Father God, are leading me to a new and wonderful future."

Study question answers found on pages 184-190

Live Again

A true story of overcoming los

Chapter 6: Creating Healing Environments on Purpose

Environments are Key

We have already examined how our environment affects our lives by affecting the decisions we make. Similarly, our environment plays a key role in the healing process of overcoming loss. My family understood this. All of them have a solid understanding of healing and the Word. One of the things they did (that at the time I regretted but later thanked them immensely for) was guard my environment. I said it before—the soul takes time adjusting to the realization that the person you love is no longer there.

The day after Marcus passed, I woke up earnestly wanting to feel, see, be a part of something that represented Marcus. I wanted to touch his clothes, smell his cologne, sit in his chair. I yearned to somehow see him. I had slept at my mom's that first night, so I quickly got dressed and went home. I ran straight to his closet only to find it empty! I fell to the ground and wept uncontrollably. The night before, while I was sleeping at my mom's, the rest of my family had cleared everything that belonged to Marcus out of our house: pictures, clothing, personal belongings, and even furniture. I was so angry; if only I could touch something of his. My mom came in the closet with me and simply held me. I don't know how long she held me in that closet. I didn't want to leave. After I had cried for a bit, she lifted me up and said, "That's enough now." She lovingly wiped the tears from my face. Being very concerned for my health, my mom would not let me go too far in my crying, because she had an understanding that a spirit of grief could easily attach itself to me in my vulnerability and try to take me out as well. It is one thing to cry and grieve the loss of someone. This is okay, but, when we go too far in our sorrow, it is possible to give our bodies over to a spirit of grief. The spirit of grief can lead to depression and feelings that you no longer want to live. I'm not saying you can't cry. Crying over the loss of someone or something is perfectly healthy and normal...to a point. I am suggesting that it is safe to limit the amount of crying you do so you don't fall into this dangerous trap.

My mother began to share why my family removed everything from the house. She explained that I would take much longer to heal if I had constant reminders of Marcus around me. With everything still there, or maybe just some of his stuff still there, I could be having a perfectly fine day, and turn the corner and see his chair, and be thrown backward in my healing process. My family removed every obstacle out of the way so I could begin the healing process and keep moving forward in it. They were led by the Lord to do this. I couldn't understand it. I was so extremely attached to Marcus. We were as one identity. I didn't know where I left off and he picked up.

Everywhere I looked I tried to find him. When I was in the kitchen, I kept looking up toward the stairwell, waiting to see him come down in his robe, but he wasn't coming. I wanted to hear his voice, his singing, his laughter.

My mind felt cloudy as if I had cotton in it. I so desperately wanted to think straight but I couldn't. I had no desire to eat or do anything. All I wanted to do was close my eyes, sleep, wake up, and have it be all right.

I knew these were all signs of depression. The pain I was experiencing was so deep, a pain I had never experienced before in my life. Several years prior, I had taught on emotional pain, explaining how everyone experiences it, but at different levels in different situations. This level seemed unbearable. In the past, the Lord had touched my physical body and relieved me of pain many times over. This was so much bigger. Now I needed to be relieved of a pain so deep in my soul.

Isaiah 53: 3-5 says, *He was despised and rejected by men, a man of sorrows and familiar with suffering. Like one from whom men hide their faces He was despised, and we esteemed Him not. Surely He took up our infirmities and carried our sorrows.*

That Hebrew word that is translated "sorrow" here literally means "pain." He carried our pain! I can remember saying, "Okay Jesus, You said that You carried my pain. This hurts. I thought You said You carried our pain?" Have you ever said that? Jesus did carry our pain, but He never said that there wasn't potential to experience pain. When the pain comes, the wonderful thing about being a Christ follower is that there are tools to help you deal with it. I had to deal with the deep pain. Only through the enabling power of God's grace was I able to deal with the deep pain.

Again, my pain was emotional, not physical. Emotional pain can seem harder to deal with than physical pain.

With physical pain it is "easy" to tell where physical pain is happening, it is in your head, arm, or leg and there are pain relievers to help treat it. Emotional pain is different. It is an aching that seems to consume everything, is difficult to even describe, let alone pinpoint where it starts or ends, and pain relievers don't make it go away.

I have had to walk with people who have gone through divorce. On the outside there wasn't an obvious sign of pain or destruction (like bruises, a cast, stitches, an oxygen machine), but on the inside, where no one could see, there were deep wounds that couldn't be stitched. I knew the pain I was experiencing wasn't going to go away on its own. I knew I had to do some things on purpose for it to go away. I had to let God work on the inside of me and sew it all back together.

The Love of God is Beyond Feeling

Even in my weakened condition, I sensed God leading me with regard too His Love for me. Looking back I understand why. When we go through a tragedy, many times we struggle with thoughts that if God really loved me, He wouldn't allow me to be going through horrific tragedy. They are lies, lies, lies! Jesus taught the parable about storms coming on two homes that were built on different foundations—one being sand, the other being rock. The sand represents a life being built independent of God. The rock represents the opposite—a life that is built dependent on God. The storm destroyed the house built on the sand, but not the one on the rock.[1] A storm had come to my life with the potential to destroy me. God didn't send the storm. Life sent the storm. The devil sent the storm. Was I going to trust God and the promises He made in His Word and remain standing? It is so easy to trust God's love for us when things are going well, but it's a whole different story when life's trials hit.

God said in His Word that I would go through the fire but not get burned.2 I felt burned. But God said I would not be burned. I had an understanding that the potential to be burned or even destroyed was there if I did not allow God to hold me and walk me through my healing. I felt burned. I felt as if I were drowning. My house felt destroyed. Yet God did not see me this way. I had a choice to side in with my feelings or side in with God. I knew my feelings would deceive me and leave me in a place of brokenness, and I knew that God, in His miraculous love, could get me to the other side.

When I felt hopeless, I remembered a saying of my mom's: "A miracle begins with a problem." She would teach that for a miracle to happen we have to believe that God can fix the problem. This is not easy to do when your feelings say, "It's hopeless." My feelings were saying, "You're alone and destitute, it's all over for you". But God was saying something else:

"The Lord is close to the brokenhearted, and saves those who are crushed in spirit" (Psalm 34:18).

Whether or not we feel it, God is close to us in our brokenhearted condition. He understands and feels with us, and He is available to save us! The word *"saves"* in the original Hebrew means "He avenges, defends, delivers, rescues, and helps those who are crushed in spirit."3 I was a prime candidate for that piece of Scripture. I needed to be rescued from the deep pain and brokenness.

I also battled with thoughts of, "I'm the only one. No one else is feeling what I'm feeling." Many struggle with this when they go through a trial. One day when I was having one of those pity parties, I received a timely phone call from a fellow minister. Her particular ministry involves much travel; consequently she is exposed to multitudes of people and their issues. She began to share with me that, within that particular month alone, how many women ministers had been widowed. God knew how to meet me where I was, and through that conversation, He showed me that I was not alone.

I had to believe that I was going to make it through this storm, that I would not drown, and I had to choose to trust His saving power. Why? Because God said He was close and able to save me! In order to stay in this place of believing and trusting God, I had to place myself-on purpose—in appropriate environments for healing. As I mentioned in previous chapters, we are shaped by our environment.

End notes:
1. Matthew 7: 24-27
2. Isaiah 43:2
3. P. C. Study Bible: Strong's Greek/Hebrew Dictionary

Questions for Chapter Six:
1. When we go too far in our sorrow, it is possible to give ourselves over to a spirit of grief. What can the spirit of grief lead to?

2. In Isaiah 53:4 the word "sorrow" means what?

3. According to this Scripture did Jesus bear our pain?

Reflect:
In the middle of your tragedy, have you questioned whether or not God loves you? Don't question! He loves you so much He sent His Son to die on a cross for you. You may be experiencing emotional pain right now. Are you ready to let God touch you?

Act:
Say, "Jesus, it says in Isaiah 53:4 that You carried my pain. What You bore I need not bear. Jesus, I receive Your touch right now. Thank You for healing the pain." Every time you feel emotional pain say, "Jesus, thank You for taking the pain."

Study question answers found on pages 184-190

Live Again

A true story of overcoming los

Chapter 7: The Presence

The love of God is the strongest force in the world and is the medicine for healing. The love of God has to be pursued. I knew it was the key to my healing, so I pursued His presence. My mom would often say, "If you spend time with Love you will become Love." In the presence of God is the Love of God. In that love there is joy, peace, comfort, strength...everything we need. Depression and grief were knocking at my door. I had a choice to either open that door or open the door of His presence.

The Holy Spirit is the Presence of God

Psalm 16:11 says, *You have made known to me the path of life. You will fill me with joy in your presence and with eternal pleasures at your right hand.*

The presence of God is the presence of the Holy Spirit. Just before Jesus was crucified, He talked with His disciples regarding the Holy Spirit. Jesus knew that the disciples would be rocked in their faith when He was taken from them. So Jesus began to introduce to them that He would still be with them, just in a different form than what they were accustomed to: a spirit form without a physical body. In Christ's physical absence the Holy Spirit would do what Christ would do if He were physically present: save, love and heal people through followers of Christ.

Jesus told His disciples that He would not leave them (and us) as orphans, but that He would come and make His home in them through the presence of the Holy Spirit. Jesus said He would never leave us or forsake us, because He knew He would take up residence in our spirit through the Holy Spirit. It's hard to believe this, because our human brains cannot wrap themselves around this concept. That's why faith in God means believing what the Bible says, even when it doesn't make sense.

I believed that the Holy Spirit was inside of me. I believed what Jesus said about Him, that the Holy Spirit was to comfort, guide, bring peace, stand by me, and be my advocate. Wherever my limits end, His power would begin! Because I believed, His power would be available to be released in my life. The Holy Spirit is a real person sent to help us. Why? Because God loves us and sees our limitations. (I acknowledge Him every day and call Him my honored Guest!) And according to His Word I could receive joy in His presence, through the Holy Spirit, and I needed to access it.

Years ago I was on vacation, walking along the beach, unaware that I was being bitten by these little bugs called no-see-ums. My trip was ruined because of them! I had a terrible itchy reaction to their bites and couldn't seem to get relief. I vowed that that would never happen again. I learned, after that encounter, that there is only one product that really safeguards against their bites. Years later, as I was just about to walk on a beach, I heard a woman say, "Oh, the no-see-ums are out." I asked her where the closest pharmacy was. She told me; however, she already knew that that store did not carry the product I needed, so she directed me to another place that was farther away. I didn't care how far I had to drive. I had to get it to ensure my safety. Likewise, I knew that according to the Word of God I had to go somewhere to get some joy. I had to go to His presence.

There's another Scripture:
Those who wait on the LORD shall renew their strength; they shall mount up with wings like eagles, they shall run and not grow weary, they shall walk and not faint (Isaiah 40:31).

The word *wait* means "to look patiently, tarry, wait for, on, upon, with an expectancy."[1] If I were to wait, then I would eventually be renewed, mount up to fly again, run without growing weary and walk without fainting. What a promise! I needed all the above. I had to run to His presence on purpose to receive whatever I needed at that moment. I had to be in that environment for healing.

There is a Transfer in His Presence

There is a transfer that occurs when we are in His presence. We exchange the negative stuff for His healing stuff. We experience similar transfers in our relationships. When my daughters sit down to talk with me, we begin to exchange words. In those words I'm building them up and we love on each other. (If you have children) you can understand that there is this transfer that happens when we communicate in this loving way. Do we physically see that transfer? No, but we have the transfer, don't we? Although we can't touch it, we know, we have experienced a transfer of each other's love.

The same thing happens when we go into the presence of God. In His presence there is a transfer of divine love that He pours into the core of our soul. I look at God as my Father. So when I went into His presence saying, "Okay, I am so broken, and I'm such a mess. I'm coming expecting a divine transfer. You said that I would receive joy in Your presence. You said that I would get strength in Your presence. Well, You see I'm a wreck, and I need You!" Whether or not I felt it, I believed that every time I was with Him there was a divine transfer that would sustain me. Now as Christ followers we have our devotional life. We get up in the morning, spend time with God, and then, throughout the day, we have conversations with Him. But, in that particular season, I had to go into my study several times a day, close the door and say "Okay, I'm back. I need Your help again. I need some more of everything You have. I'm drowning again." He was so faithful. He is so very faithful.

The Enemy Takes Advantage of Our Weakened Condition

It was not easy going into God's presence. Many times I wanted to just wallow in my sorrow. I wanted to feel sorry for myself and host a big old pity party. But I had to go into His presence whether I felt like it or not. I had been taught that feelings are indicators, not facts or the absolute truth. The Bible is the Truth. When I went into my study again, I reminded myself and God, of His promises as I ignored my feelings. (I am not saying that we have to always ignore our feelings, but there is a point when we need to use reason and keep ourselves from falling into a big pit.)

I was warned by pastors in my life that the devil would

try to take advantage of my weakened condition. I was familiar with what they were saying because of an experience I'd had several years prior when Marcus and I were first married. We were living in this cute little place and I had no reason to be sad. Everything was going so great for me. However, this one day while I was walking through our home doing a few things, I suddenly began to feel so depressed, as if I had no reason to live. Have you ever felt that? It came out of nowhere and it was getting stronger and stronger. I kept thinking, "I should be ecstatic! I have a great husband, a wonderful, cozy apartment, a great future ahead of me. Why am I experiencing depression?"

During this particular season of my life I was pursuing and learning how to discern God's voice. As I've said in previous chapters, we are created to hear our Heavenly Father's voice. We simply need to train our ear to His language. His language is the Word of God. If you relocate to a foreign country you have to train your ear to discern new syllables and sounds to learn the language, and so it is with God's voice. As we consistently spend time with Him and His Word we will develop an ear to hear His voice. And we should all strive to hear from Him.

Because I had been learning how to discern God's voice, I knew that the small voice I was hearing was God, even in the midst of those feelings of depression. It wasn't like a booming, "THUS SAYETH THE LORD," in a Charlton Heston-like biblical movie voice with smoke and thunder. No! It was nothing like that. It was very subtle. He said, "This is a spirit of depression. That's all it is. Just start to worship Me. Start to praise Me and it will leave."

I put in a Worship CD and began to worship God saying, "I'm so grateful You are in my life. I am so thankful that I'm saved, and You are my Lord." I continued for about twenty minutes and then, "poof!" that spirit of depression lifted. I knew then that the Lord was teaching me something.

Sometimes when we experience a spirit of grief or depression (or really any negative emotion), it seems so much a part of who we are that we really think it is a part of us, but the truth is that it's something from the pit of hell that is taking advantage of our vulnerability. People say, "I just feel so depressed." Maybe it's not them; maybe it's something else. I realized that day that a simple twenty minutes of nothing big, nothing loud or obnoxious, just my saying, "Lord, I love You. I praise You. I thank You," can lift oppression. I didn't feel like worshiping or thanking God when that depression spirit hit. Who wants to worship when you're going through something like that? However, because I heard His still small voice, I understood that if I would insert myself into His presence, if I would worship Him when I didn't feel like worshiping, those negative spirits had to leave.

Years later I was to experience this same thing again, right after Marcus passed. The negative spirits had to leave again. Had I not been aware of how negative spirits work, I would have thought that those feelings were just "me" and simply accept them, and they would have destroyed me.

It was not always easy to go into God's presence. Often it was a fight, but it was always worth it. I'm so grateful for the strength of the Holy Spirit, always there to help us in our weaknesses!

Many times when I would be in His presence I would just want to cry. I would often worship with tears streaming down my face. I would cry for so long, and then I would again sense the Holy Spirit prompting me to stop. One day, I was really going back to the past, to the "What if's," and I sensed the Holy Spirit say, "You don't need to go there. All of that is past. There's no healing for you back there. I want you to look to your future for your healing. Tracy, where do you want to go?" I knew at that moment, out of God's great love for me, He would follow me wherever I decided to go, because He said He would never leave me or forsake me. I yielded to His prompt-ings, decided to move forward into healing, and received His touch again.

It was in His presence that a great transfer of what I needed on that day, of what I needed at that moment, was made. To this day, I cannot explain the comfort and relief I experienced in His presence. I have often described it as a "bubble" around me, with my being so safe and so secure in the middle. I was fully aware that He was with me, and I felt so humbled that my God was that close with me at that moment, and He wants to be that close to you too.

End notes:
1. PC Study Bible: Strong's Greek/Hebrew Dictionary

Questions for Chapter 7:
1. The presence of God is the presence of the
_____?

2. According to Psalm 16:11, what can we find in His presence?

3. According Isaiah 40:31, what happens when we "wait" upon the Lord?

4. There is a transfer that occurs in His presence; we exchange_____.

Reflect:
With the onslaught of a tragedy/loss, have you battled with depression? Has it felt as if it has become a part of you? Have you become accustomed to those feelings? If so, it's time to go to God. It's time to access His presence. Depression left unchecked will destroy your life. You have a lot more life in you!

Act:
Purpose to spend some daily time in conversations with God so that you can access His presence. Allow God to transfer His healing touch to you. As you wait on God, say, "God, You are renewing my strength according to Isaiah 40:31. I will run and not grow weary. I will walk and not faint."

Study question answers found on pages 184-190

Chapter 8: His Word

Our Soul Needs Medicine

I knew I had to immerse myself in the Word of God in order to get my healing. I spent a lot of time in environments where the Word was being taught, such as Bible studies and Bible classes. I listened to teaching CD's. Again, I recognized those environments were breeding grounds for my healing, and I purposed to surround myself with them.

Also, I knew that in the natural, when we have an ailment, like an infection, we go to doctors and they give us an antibiotic. Generally, when we take an antibiotic, we believe, "Okay, in about a day or two, for sure by three, I'm just going to be feeling great." We take that antibiotic with the full assurance that we're going to be fine, don't we? We don't even think about it. In fact, we trust the antibiotic so much that we will even plan an outing later. We are sure that we are going to be fine, because we believe in the power of that medicine. It's the same with the soul. As I have said before, it is our soul (mind, will and emotions) that needs healing when we go through a tragedy—it is our soul that needs medicine.

First Thessalonians 5:23 reveals that we are made of three parts:

May God himself, the God of peace [He's not a

God of Strife, He's not a God of Confusion], sanctify you through and through. May your whole spirit, soul and body be kept blameless at the coming of our Lord Jesus Christ.
[Emphasis added by the author in brackets.]

This Scripture separates our being into a spirit, a soul, and a body. When we become a Christ follower our spirit is reunited with our heavenly Father and at that moment our spirit looks just like the image of God. He calls us His children. He is not only Lord and Savior, but Father—a Father who is absolutely crazy about us! If you've been abused by your Father, you may not be able, at this point, to see God in a fatherly way, but in time, as you get to know Him as your wonderful Savior and Lord, your image of father will be healed.

I had to ask the Lord to let me see Him as Father, because I didn't have the greatest relationship with my own earthly father. He's a great guy but we just didn't have a great relationship. He came from the old country and didn't really know how to have that kind of relationship with me. His mentality, based on his own life experience, was so completely different from mine, that I really didn't understand the nurturing that comes from a father, because I hadn't experienced it personally. But when I became a Christ follower, God began to lead me down a path to see Him as my loving Father. How? He began to place strong, fatherly men in my life, for specific seasons, to mentor me in things that pertained to being a woman. In fact, during college, I spent a year living with a pastor, his wife and their children, and that pastor hovered over me like a dad. All four years that I was in college this wonderful family took me under its wings, and I was able to witness firsthand how a healthy husband and father treated his wife and children.

He's a Father to the Fatherless

God in His mercy did that for me because, as He said in His Word in Psalm 68:5, "He is a father to the fatherless." How does He do that? He will send people along our paths. We, however, have to receive that grace in our lives. He will make up the difference for that lack. Many times God is sending those relational figures that we lacked in the past into our lives, but we are not seeing them as a God-send because we keep focusing on the fact that we lacked those relationships. Unfortunately we miss the potential to heal. Maybe the person sent to make up the lack, or redeem your situation, isn't what you expected, but one thing is for sure, they will be touched by God to minister to your precise needs and they will fill the lack in specific areas of your life. Throughout my life, God, in His love, placed people in my path from the Body of Christ (the Church) to make up for what I lacked. He is so good. That is the God we can call Father. He is a God of grace and a God of mercy Who loves to make up the difference.

God Wants to Heal and Transform Our Soul

I have realized that my whole walk with God has resulted in the healing and transforming of my soul. My spirit was whole the moment I became a Christ-follower. It has been my soul that has taken time to be healed and transformed. The potential is there to be conformed into the image of my heavenly Father, but it is a process.

Our soul needs healing when we go through emotional tragedy and I knew this. James 1:21 NKJV says, *There-*

fore lay aside all filthiness, overflow of wickedness, and receive with meekness the implanted word which is able to save your souls. This word, *save* means "to heal, preserve, save, do well, and make your soul whole."1 So what is this Scripture saying? It's telling us that there is this medicinal power in the Word of God that when we put it (the Word, the medicine) in our mouth and in our heart, it gets into our soul and is able to save, able to preserve it and make it whole. My soul needed a lot of help, and according to James 1:21, when I put this Word into me, it had the power to heal and deliver my soul. God just needed for me to believe it.

Many times I read the Word but didn't feel any better. Has that ever happened to you? Listen, we can't go by our feelings. Just as it takes time for that antibiotic to work, it takes time for the Word to work too. If we are consistent with our medication we will see results. Isn't that true? Likewise, if we are consistent with the Word coming into our soul, we will see results. Have you ever not finished a prescription and, as a result didn't get over the illness, and then had to go back and get another prescription? I have been guilty of that. Is the fact that I didn't get better the medicine's fault or my fault?

Do we always enjoy taking medicine? Sometimes it tastes bad, it can be hard to swallow, or bother our stomach, but we need to take it nonetheless. So whether I felt like it or not, I kept showing up in His presence through His Word, believing His medicine was infusing my soul and bringing healing.

End notes:
1. PC Study Bible: Strong's Greek/Hebrew Dictionary

Questions for Chapter 8:
1. In James 1:21 what does the word *save* mean?

2. As an antibiotic is medicine to the body, so the Word (Bible) is _____ to the soul.

Reflect:
Have you read the Bible and felt absolutely nothing? Just because you felt nothing doesn't mean that something did not happen to your soul and body. It's time to believe that every time you are in the Bible your soul is receiving the medicine it needs.
Say, "Father, I believe that every time I am reading and saying Your Word, Your healing power is coming into my soul. James 1:21 tells me to receive this Word because it is able to save my soul. I believe You are healing and preserving my soul."

Act:
Right now, purpose to spend time daily in the Bible, allowing continual healing to manifest in your soul. Start with the Book of John or a chapter of Proverbs a day. Before you read, ask God to enlighten your spiritual eyes to know and understand Him.

Study question answers found on pages 184-190

Live Again

A true story of overcoming los

Chapter 9: The Love of God

During the initial season after Marcus' passing, the Scriptures that I felt led to read were from the books of 1, 2 and 3 John. These three books of the Bible focus on the love of God. I kept reading about the love of God and began to understand that God wanted to fill my soul with His love. You see God is love, and He wanted me to fill my whole being with His love. He wanted me to grow in my understanding of the greatness and completeness of His love. The Scripture I focused on the most was 1 John 4:18, *"There is no fear in love. But perfect love drives out fear."*

God's Love Casts Out Fear!

In those first few months I battled tremendous fear. I found myself battling thoughts like, "Will I ever feel again? Can I ever be normal? Will I ever have a real life again? Will my kids ever be normal or will they be scarred? Will they be damaged by not having a father? Will they ever have a father again? What am I going to do?" All of those squirrelly thoughts, that are very common to have when you suffer a loss, were going through my brain.

We need to remember that God understands how we are made. He understands how vulnerable we can be when we are under attack and that Scripture, "perfect love casts out fear" reveals that God's love can cast out fear. So I had to start saying this promise, and I had to start seeing my life through this promise. I began to say, "God, since You love me, You have a great future for me. God, since You love me, You are going to heal me. God, since You love me, my kids are going to be fine. God, since You love me, there's a future and hope, even though right now I can't see it. You said that You love me. So, since You love me, You are already going ahead of me now and taking care of everything that concerns me." I had to say that. I didn't feel like it was happening, and I didn't see it right away, but that was His promise, so I *chose* to believe it. I walked around the house and simply said, "You love me, God; You love me! And because You love me everything is going to be okay." What was happening, as I purposed to say this, was that I was allowing myself to receive a supernatural impartation of God's love. That Scripture, "Perfect love casts out fear" (1 John 4:18) was medicine for my soul, and I took a dose of it regularly and trusted that it would be effective in healing me.

Saying, "God, You love me. Your perfect love casts out all fear," was equal to an antibiotic going inside me, doing a tremendous unseen work. As I was committed to saying this, God was reassuring me saying, "I love you, Tracy. I have everything under control. I know baby girl, you can't see one thing right now. I know you are so broken that you can't even fathom one thing. Still, I love you, Tracy. I love you, Tracy." That love is so powerful. To this day, I am living in that love.

That season was so precious because I gained the understanding that no matter what I face in life, His love repels and destroys any fear that will ever come against me! I have experienced the carrying power of His love, and although I am trying to convey its enormity right now, it can't be put to words! It is my life's ambition that everybody I meet would experience this love that can only be received in your spirit by Him. No man can do it. No person, man, woman, or child can fill the empty space that is left when one passes, but God's love can. It is that powerful!

I found out that God is not complicated. In fact, He is very simple. I simply had to say, "God, You love me, and You have everything under control, even though it doesn't look like it." That was the secret to my healing! Isn't that amazing? One verse about God's love was so powerful, because the love of God is the strongest force in the earth. Why do you think there are so many sub-stitutes for it? Why do you think the enemy has people so busy with counterfeits of love? The enemy says, "Oh, let me keep them so preoccupied and busy with coun-terfeits of love, let me keep them so distracted that they can't tap into the real love of God, because if they tap into the real love of God, I'll lose them."

God's Love Changes our Outlook

The Love of God became so real on the inside of me, it began to change my whole outlook on life and I am still impacted today. I see life in such a positive way.

Because I am an associate pastor, I hear about all sorts of horrible situations that people face in their lives. As people tell me their terrible stories, they expect me to freak out, but I look at them and simply ask, "And? Is God not bigger than that?" The love of God changes your outlook. You begin to have a whole new perspective on life—one that is fresh and full of potential because the love of God is full of potential. God's love is filled with future. It's full of hope. I was ingesting love, so I was full of hope, full of future, and full of potential. Sometimes, a hundred times a day, I would walk through my house saying, "You love me. Oh, You love me God." As soon as a negative thought would come concerning one of my three girls being dysfunctional due to the loss, I would say, "You love me God. No, no, the girls' future, that's Your problem, not mine. Now, You are their Father. You. You are going to take care of them." I would say that. Anyone who looked through my window might have thought I was nuts, because I was talking to myself so much. You can't just "think away" squirrelly thoughts. You can't. As soon as they come, you have to get rid of them, because if you entertain them long enough, they become what you believe and expect. When they come, you have to deal with them immediately and speak to them. You have to say, "No, I'm not going down there! God loves me, and His love casts out all fear."

If we don't fill ourselves with His Word of healing for our soul, we will fill it with something else by default. We won't remain empty. We have to purpose to fill ourselves up with His Word that brings life and healing. Whatever we fill ourselves up with will shape who we are.

God's Love is Experienced

Another wonderful Scripture that I want to share with you is Ephesians 3:16-19. I love these verses! These particular Scriptures were actually a prayer that the Apostle Paul prayed for the church in his day. When we pray these Scriptures today, they are just as powerful as when they were prayed way back then. As Christ-followers, we can take them for our own lives and receive the promises for ourselves. Ephesians 3, beginning in

verse 16, says, *I pray that out of His glorious riches, He may strengthen you with power through His spirit in your inner being....* [Do you see the divine transfer? Through His Spirit in your inner being, the transfer of power that strengthens us happens.] *So that Christ may dwell in your hearts through faith. And I pray that you, being rooted and established in love, may have power, together with all the saints, to grasp how wide and long and high and deep is the love of Christ, and to know this love that surpasses knowledge...*
[Emphasis added by the author in brackets.]

I know that I will spend the rest of my life searching the love of God and still not understand it completely. I know my understanding will grow more and more each day as I seek His love, but I will never know it all. It is truly that wide, that high, that long and that deep. This verse says we can know God's love and that it "surpasses knowledge." Think about that. God's love is so big, it surpasses knowledge, and though we might never reach understanding completely, we can know it!

This word *know* means not just to know about love as a concept in your head, but to *experience* it. We can experience that love! This love is an intimate word. We experience that intimate love with our spouses. The love we share with them is a deeper, more personal love than we share with any other person.

Another example of this love is the love we have for our children. It is impossible for me to describe my love for my kids. It is beyond words. It doesn't even always make sense. Even when my kids are disobedient and I feel like I want to scream, even in that moment, if someone or something came against them, I would defend them. I would do anything for my kids. Anything! And yet God loves me more than that. I can't understand that. It's beyond my ability to understand.

Ephesians 3:19 continues on to say, *and to know this love that surpasses knowledge—that you may be filled to the measure of all the fullness of God.* Well, if God is love, and I'm receiving His love, then I'm being filled with the fullness of God. No wonder God took me to that Scripture, "Perfect love of God casts out all fear," because He was trying to show me, "Tracy, fill yourself up with this love. It will surpass anything and everything in your life." It was my pill, and it can be your pill as well. I could spend a lifetime talking about the love of God. It's amazing, as soon as you finish peeling off one layer of understanding, there is another and another and another!

As we seek His love and experience it, more and more of the love of God is transferred to us. When I talk to a close friend on the phone, and I encourage and love on them, they receive my love even though we are communicating by phone. I didn't touch my friend physically, yet there was a transfer. It's the same thing with God. In our dialogue with Him, there is a transfer of love that we have the privilege and the honor to receive, and that love is healing.   It's amazing!

Questions for Chapter 9:
1. What is able to cast out fear?

2. If we don't fill ourselves with His Word of healing for our soul, by default we will fill it with _____ else.

3. What is one of the ways we can receive God's love?

Reflect:
Have you battled fearful thoughts, as I did, such as, "Will I ever feel again? Can I ever be normal? Will I ever have a real life again?" The answer to all of these questions is YES! God's love is the antidote for fearful thoughts. God's love must be received:

Say, "Father, You said in 1 John 4:18 that Your Love drives out fear. I receive Your love. I believe Your love is driving out all the fear that rises up in me."

You see, fear will rise up; thoughts will come. Speak to them. They will leave and the love will come.

Act:
Commit to memory 1 John 4:18.
When you start your day, begin saying out loud, "God, You love me. I refuse to fear. You have a great future for me, because You love me." Every time you have a fearful thought say it again, again and again, until the thought leaves.

Live Again

A true story of overcoming los

Chapter 10: The Body of Christ

As iron sharpens iron, so one man sharpens another.
                                        —(Proverbs 27:17)

When I was growing up, my mom used to say, "Tell me who you go with, and I will tell you who you will become." She knew that those we allow into our lives and surround ourselves with shapes who we become. Proverbs 27:17 reflects that people in our lives should sharpen us (encouraging us to be better people) and not tear us down. With this understanding in mind, I was very careful about who I allowed into my life during my season of healing from Marcus' passing. I was doing all I could to keep myself in a healing environment, and this included monitoring conversations and input from people. I was aware that one conversation with a person who was negative could pull me down and destroy much of the work I had done.

One day, shortly after Marcus passed, I took my kids to our community pool, and a woman who had heard about what had happened approached me. She broke down crying, and she was clinging to me saying, "I'm so sorry, I'm so sorry!" I remember thinking, "Wow, grief is all over her." It was really strange, because I felt like I had to comfort her! I kept thinking, "What is wrong with this picture?" The grief that was on her was trying to come on me. I was fully aware that in this encounter I was surrounded by God's presence. I knew I was in the "bubble." I was insulated and at peace, and she was a mess. I was also aware that if I remained there, being bombarded by that grief, that I would be negatively affected. I politely excused myself, and from that point on, I was extra cautious about those I allowed into my realm of influence.

There were phone calls that I would not receive, because I knew that those particular people could not help me in that moment, but could only bring me to a place of fear and acceptance of grief. Until I was strong enough, I had to do this. I had worked so hard, on purpose, to get into His presence, to have His bubble protecting me, so that I could heal. I knew that I had to, on purpose, keep people from popping my bubble.

Surround Yourself with People Who are Strong

On purpose, I surrounded myself with people who were strong in God—people who were full of faith and who would speak God's encouraging promises to me. It was another part of my environment that promoted healing. I am so thankful for the Body of Christ, specifically for the members at my church, Life Christian Church. They did not see me as a poor, grieving widow, but they saw me as a woman whom God would heal completely. They saw me as a woman who would have a great future, a woman who would continue to be brought from glory to glory, a woman whose life God was totally willing and able to redeem from everything the enemy had planned for her destruction. That's how they spoke to me, and about me, and that is what they believed when they prayed for me.

So many times while I was walking through my home I was aware that someone was praying for me. (Our church is strong on the teaching of prayer and our members are praying people who get results). In their love for me, they prayed. They are responsible, in part for my healing. The church you attend is so important. The quality of teaching you receive from your church plays a large part of shaping who you are.

I am forever grateful for Life Christian Church. They lovingly stood by me, prayed for me continually, and truly believed with expectancy that I would heal. They saw me with a terrific future in the middle of the chaos and wouldn't let anything but those terrific promises pass through their lips.

Chapter 10 Questions:

1. In our time of healing we need to be surrounded by people who are strong in the Lord—who will _____ us and not tear us down.

2. Does it matter what church you attend? Why?

Reflect:

Are the people surrounding you building you up or tearing you down? It is very easy to fall into the "woe is me" mode when we are around people who let us wallow. It's hard to stay positive in the wake of a tragedy, therefore, choose wisely whom you are spending your time with. Make sure you are being encouraged.

Act:

If you are not a part of a spiritually healthy church body, search for one and get plugged in. Those relationships will help in the healing process. Make sure their core beliefs fit what you believe. Read Hebrews 10:25:
Let us not give up meeting together, as some are in the habit of doing, but let us encourage one another—and all the more as you see the Day approaching.

Study question answers found on pages 184-190

Chapter 11: Call It Different

As you have seen already, during my healing process, I had to say a lot of things that were contrary to what I was feeling or seeing. I learned long ago in my Christian walk that feelings are indicators, not leaders. My senses are great until they try to lead me contrary to God's Word. I've also learned that since I am made in the image of God, I have an ability to create through my words.

Adam and Eve, in the original creation, were told to subdue the earth and to rule over it. Those words are powerful. Together those words mean "to bring into subjection and reign over."[1] This was their assignment over the earth, because God made them "little" rulers under God, or ambassadors, over the earth. How were they supposed to fulfill their assignment? The same way their heavenly Father did, through their spoken words. God spoke, and things happened. He said, "Let there be light" and there was light. It happened. He didn't just think it; He spoke it. Likewise, when we speak, things happen because we are made in His image with a creative ability in our words. There are so many patterns and clues about this in the Bible. One in particular is Proverbs 18:21: *The tongue has the power of life and death and those who love it will eat of its fruit.*

What we say can create either positive or negative results in our lives. Science has proven this as well. I was reading about this in a wonderful book called **The**

Fourth Dimension by Paul Yonggi Cho. The book tells of a time when the author was having lunch with a well-known neurosurgeon. The surgeon was sharing all his findings regarding how the speech center of the brain rules over, and has total dominion over, all the nerves. He shared that when a human being says something, the nervous system sets out to do it. It's almost as if the words spoken were their marching orders and they set out to accomplish them. He went on to give examples. One was of a person who retired from his job and continued to say, "I'm retired." His whole body began to agree and perform what he had said. Thus the retiree began to experience his body going into retirement and shutting down...symptoms of retirement! Dr. Cho basically said that what this surgeon had told him was something that he had already known from the Bible![2]

I understood these concepts and realized how important it was that I spoke what God's Word said regarding me and my future. God's Word said to me:
"I know the plans I have for you declares the Lord. Plans to prosper you and not to harm you. Plans to give you hope and a future" (Jeremiah 29:11). It didn't feel like a hope, and it didn't look like a future. It didn't seem like it at all! How can there be a future and a hope here? You see, in my mind the only future and hope I wanted was Marcus. Obviously that wasn't available, so despite what my mind was thinking I would say, "You said I have a future, God. You said it. I don't know how You're going to do it, but You said it, so I am going to believe it." Marcus was the only hope and future I could see. But in that moment, when I couldn't see, I trusted God. I put all my faith and belief in the fact that He could see and that He knew exactly what a hope and a future would look like for me. He already had the whole situ-

couldn't see, I trusted God. I put all my faith and belief in the fact that He could see and that He knew exactly what a hope and a future would look like for me. He already had the whole situation figured out. I just needed to look to Him so that I could see it too.

And we know that in all things God works for the good for those who love Him and who have been called according to His purpose (Romans 8:28).

 I looked at that Scripture quite a bit and thought, "How can things work together for good in this situation? He's dead." It sure didn't feel like good. It certainly didn't look like good. "How can any good come out of death? How can death be turned around?" I had those thoughts. And though those thoughts are very natural, I couldn't stay there. I had to say, "But God, You said that good was going to come out of this situation. I can't fathom how. I don't know how, but You said it, so I believe it, and I expect to see it."

Most of the time I'd be saying those Scriptures with tears rolling down my face. It was not an easy road. It wasn't. But in it, there was a grace. Just as my mom had picked me up in that closet, saying, "Okay, baby, that's enough," God did that to me many times. He would say to me, "Okay, you've cried enough, Tracy." Every day I would say, "Here I am again, God," and I would say those Scriptures and worship Him. I knew eventually that the medicine of God's Word would kick in.3 I knew that this Word which was able to save me would eventually do something to my soul.

That is such a key in healing: believing that no matter what you feel and no matter what it looks like God is working. God is working! He promised that His Word would not return void without accomplishing what it has been sent to do.4 His Word works. It was not my job to understand how it works. It was my job to trust that it would work.

Faith is: Believing, Trusting, and Clinging to God's Word

This is what faith really is: believing, trusting, and clinging to what God's Word says about your life over what it looks or feels like. Faith doesn't use our senses as facts and is quite often contrary to our senses. Our senses are great until they declare something contrary to what God is saying. It is impossible to have this kind of faith without a consistency in God's Word. God's Word is His character. We gain faith in a person based on observing how he acts, through his words and actions. Over a period of time we begin to trust his character. It is the same with God. As we grow in understanding Him, our faith in Him grows.

Our Faith in God allows us to access unseen supernatural heavenly realities and to bring them into our natural existence. Because we are a spirit connected to the Spirit of Christ, we have access. Faith is not needed in heaven. Faith is needed here, for it is the bridge that brings heaven's realities into our natural situations.

Have you ever seen, perhaps in a movie, when a dam bursts open? When you see it burst forth, you don't see the little crack that started at the bottom. You don't see how many little taps it took before the dam exploded. That's how it is, every time we declare a healing promise, every time we thank God for healing us, every time we worship. We are tapping the dam of our healing. The process is happening even though we can't see it or feel it, but it's happening, and someday it will burst forth in all its manifested fullness!

Abraham Spoke and Impossible Things Happened

The story of Abraham in the book of Genesis reflects this concept so well. Abraham's original name was Abram. God entered Abram's life giving him a promise that through his seed the whole world would be blessed.5 (Through this promise God was foretelling how the Christ would come as a human being through the genealogy of Abraham. What a promise!) He was seventy-five years old when God spoke this to him. Years went by and there was still no baby, so Abram made a couple of maneuvers to make the promise happen by himself, but they didn't work. To paraphrase Genesis 17-20, one day God appeared to Abram and He said, "Abram, I'm going to do My covenant with you. I'm going to do what I said I was going to do through you. You are going to have a child and all of the nations of the world are going to be blessed through your children. Your children are going to be like the stars in the heavens." In fact, there is one passage of Scripture where God actually took Abram outside and said, "Look at the stars. If you are able to number them so shall your descendents be."6 There are a lot of stars out there, and at this point of the story, nothing had happened in Abram's life. Nothing! I can just imagine Abram thinking, "How about just one baby? Just one! Just one!" Finally, God appeared to him again when he was ninety-nine years old and said to him, "I want to change your name from Abram to Abraham, which means "father of many." (Remember at this point he had zero children!) And God told Sarai, Abram's wife, that her new name was Sarah, which means "mother of many." They agreed.

I'm pretty sure they struggled with thoughts, "People are going to think we are crazy calling ourselves 'father and mother of many' when we don't even have one child and when we are way too old to have children." Abraham was well known, wealthy, and a man high in society with many employees. Can you imagine the snickers and the looks from those looking on at them as they heard Sarah say, "Father of many, it's time to eat?" Probably all the servants were saying, "They're getting up there in age. They've lost it. Senility is surely setting in." But Abraham and Sarah kept saying it. "Mother of many, is the meat cooked yet?" All would hear them introduce themselves saying, "Hi, I'm father of many." "Hi, and I'm Mother of many." People probably asked, "So how many children do you have?" Sarah would respond, "Well, none at the moment." How foolish it must have looked and felt.

Now you really have to believe God to do something like that, because we have a lot of pride. All of us do. We all care what people think about us, about how we look and sound. Three months later, Sarah conceived at 90 years old! It took three months of hearing and saying "father of many; mother of many" before something began to germinate on the inside of them. And God said, "Now I've got some faith I can work with," and they had a child in their old age.

Every Time We Speak, Something is Happening

I believe that every time I said, "God, You love me. Your perfect love casts out all fear. I have a glorious future," something was stirring on the inside of me. I wrote in my journal every month about things that were happening to me. I remember the specific time and place where I knew a healing had happened in my soul.

My mother, who is also my senior pastor, asked me to go check out our youth ministry and give her a report of what was happening. Up until this point, I was not doing anything in the ministry. It was my job to heal. I really didn't want to go and didn't think I would see nor do anything that would matter, but I went anyway. (Prior to Marcus' illness, a primary function of mine in the ministry was to grow various departments in the ministry, to locate the needs and fill them.) I walked over to the youth center with a pad of paper (which is a miracle in itself) and sat down to observe.

All of a sudden, I sensed something opening up in my soul and I saw the problems. I saw the holes, and I knew how to fix them! I saw it! I knew a part of my soul had healed. This healing happened after three months of declaring God's promises over my life! It was after three months of saying what God had told Abraham to say that Sarah had conceived. Oh, the power of saying the Word of God! Romans 4:17 says, *"...The God who gives life to the dead and calls things that are not as though they were."*

God told Abraham to call it different than what he saw and to call it the way God saw it. Why? Because we are made in His image, and we have creativity in our words! I had to agree with God as well and call it different than what my senses declared. It is so easy to call it the way it is. It takes effort to call it different. My mom would often tell us that it is so easy to be defeated, that anybody can do that, however, to succeed takes effort.

I had to declare, "God, You love me. Your perfect love casts out all fear. God, because You love me, I have a glorious future, and the girls have a glorious future, too. God, because You love me, You are healing me. God, thank You for loving me." That seed of God's Word grew in me day by day. It was three months after continually declaring God's promise that healing began to manifest in my soul.

End notes:
1. P. C. Study Bible: Strong's Greek/Hebrew Dictionary
2. Yongii Cho, Fourth Dimension, pp. 67-68.
3. Proverbs 4:22
4. Isaiah 55:11
5. Genesis 12:1-3
6. Genesis 15:5 (NKJV)

Questions to Chapter 11
1. We shared in this chapter regarding calling things different. It's not very easy to do this. Why is this so?

2. How long did Abraham and Sarah call things different before they saw a change?

Reflect:
Your words are powerful. Your words are a key in your healing process. It's time to start calling your situation different. Make a decision right now that you're going to start saying what you want to be, not what actually is. Make a decision to side in with what God is saying about you instead of your senses and circumstances.

Act:
Say "Father, in Jesus' Name, I believe You are healing me right now. You said life and death are in the power of my tongue, therefore I speak words of life. Your Word is medicine to my soul. You have a wonderful future for me because You love me." (See Proverbs 18: 21, Proverbs 4:22, Jeremiah 29:11).

Study question answers found on pages 184-190

Live Again

A true story of overcoming los

Chapter 12: Authority over Negative Influences

Have you ever come to a point in your life where you knew you had reached your limit? When you just couldn't take it anymore and you knew you needed help? A few days before Marcus passed, I walked into his hospital room and saw that he had taken a turn for the worse. He was struggling to even breathe. Immediately, I wanted to run out of there! Fear gripped me, latched onto me, and I didn't want Marcus to see it. Fear is a real thing. It's not a figment of an imagination, an idea a person's mind just makes up. It is real. I can only describe what I experienced. I felt as if there was something that grabbed onto my neck and it was preventing me from breathing. I walked out of the room for a second. I felt as if I were going to faint. I had reached my limit! I had never experienced that level of fear and anxiety prior to that moment. I realize now it was because I could not imagine my own life, for one second, without Marcus. When I saw him in that bed struggling to breathe, I knew he was going to die.

My mind was very squirrelly as I frantically phoned my family and demanded that they come that second. I screamed, "I need you! NOW!" In other instances, when I was with Marcus, I would request that they come but would often say, "If you can't come, I understand. We're here. We're fine." Not this time. They came immediately.

They knew I had reached my limit. Fear coming over me like that was something that I had never experienced before. For the first time in my life, I was face to face with a true spirit of fear. Fear grips you and it is there to kill you. Obviously, I was coming into an awareness that Marcus was leaving me. My soul could not imagine life without him. The fear of not having him consumed me.

We're all going to face times where we are fearful, weakened, or vulnerable, especially when we are going through a loss. There is tremendous potential in those moments to get into all kinds of crazy imaginations. I want to be as transparent as possible with you: don't fall for the lie that because I am a pastor that this whole season was just a walk in the park for me, because, it truly was a fight for life!

My family did come that day, not just to console me, but to pray over me. They prayed in Jesus' Name for the spirit of fear to leave me, and I got relief!

We Have the Right to Resist Negative Things

Another major point of my continued healing is based on the knowledge I was taught through God's Word, that Jesus purchased my right to resist and overcome anything destructive and negative that would enter my life. We see through Christ's life and ministry what He has provided for us through His death on the cross and resurrection.

Many have heard about Jesus being tempted by Satan. According to Luke's gospel, chapter four verse one, just after the Holy Spirit fell upon Him, Jesus was led into the wilderness for forty days without food. After the forty days, Satan came to tempt Him. (Interesting how Satan came when Jesus was in a weakened condition). Jesus was tempted three times. One of the temptations was for Jesus to worship Satan and in exchange Satan would give Jesus all the kingdoms of the world:

And he (Satan) said to him, "I will give you all their authority and splendor, for it has been given to me, and I can give it to anyone I want to. So if you worship me, it will all be yours" (Luke 4:6-7).

Notice it says in verse 6, "It's been given to me and I can give it..." Who gave Satan authority over the earth? Adam. We read in chapter 11 how Adam and Eve were given ruler-ship over the earth.1 In other words, they were ambassadors under God. God's plan was for this new creation, mankind, to eventually leave the Garden, reclaiming the earth that was inhabited by Satan.2

The Garden was a place of training, of growing, and for repopulating the earth with more "man creatures" being made in the image of God with ruling power and authority, in order to reclaim the earth. The Garden was a perfect world in the middle of an imperfect earth.

We've shared in chapter 3, that mankind listened to the temptation of Satan and didn't side with or listen to God. Adam ushered in sin and its effects. Jesus came to restore man to his original position in and with God. The Bible calls Jesus the Second Adam,3 because He was as Adam was in the Garden prior to The Fall. Unlike Adam, however, Jesus overcame the temptation of Satan. Jesus dealt with the sin issue on the cross, removing the bridge that separated us from God and our original position of authority. Once we receive Christ we are in a position to resist the negative, destructive things of the devil and overcome those situations in our lives! And Jesus will return again to overthrow and disarm Satan completely, removing him from the earth once and for all. Until then, God has given us tools to overcome.

Satan Seeks to Destroy

Now notice this: did anybody prevent the devil from tempting the Son of God, the Christ? Did anybody prevent the devil from approaching Christ and putting up a stumbling block? No. No one can prevent Satan from trying. We can't prevent such activity of the adversary in this earth, because it is fallen and he is a ruler of it. He still has power by means of operating through men and women who are cooperating with him through ignorance. The Bible says that Satan, the god of this world, blinds the minds of unbelievers.4 There are times, however, that we can prevent his plans of destruction through prayer and taking our rightful authority.

Jesus Used the Word

In Jesus' weakened condition, during the temptation in the wilderness, the weapon or tool that Jesus used was the Word of God. Jesus said three times in response to Satan's temptation, "It is written." He didn't take out a gun. He didn't take out a knife. He didn't argue or repeat himself. He simply spoke the Word out of His mouth.

Let me ask you a question: If a negative opposition didn't exist, would we need laws and boundaries? Police officers have a badge of authority to use against those who are opposing or challenging the laws and harming the public. They enforce the laws of the land to ensure the safety and good of the people.

Here's another question: Does the mob have power? Yes. We know they do because we see their destructive activity. But, do they have authority? No. They don't have authority, but they do have power.

Because a negative force will always try to get away with something, we need an authority in place to say, "No. You're crossing a boundary you're not allowed to cross." But if you take out all the negative forces...if you take out the devil...you have nothing to oppose, right? You don't need a badge of authority do you? But there is a negative force trying to oppose us. Jesus gave us authority because there is a powerful being who is challenging anything that is good! When the enemy comes against us, we have been given the privilege to use God's Word though the Name of Jesus to resist him.

Jesus Resisted Satan as a Man

Jesus resisted Satan in the authority that was given to man in Genesis 1:26-28 (bottom line paraphrase: subdue, rule, have authority over the earth). Again, Jesus was as Adam was in the Garden before he (Adam) fell. The Word was the boundary, the law, the stopping ground. Jesus, in essence, was saying, "You can't cross this. I'm in authority here." Jesus was walking under that law and that dominion, and Satan knew it. So the devil came and tried to use the Word against Jesus. But Jesus knew the Word both in and out of context. He enforced His rights, doing exactly what He was supposed to do, according to Genesis 1:26-28.

The Devil Seeks Opportune Times

The Bible says that the devil left Him (Jesus) until another opportune time.5 This tells me that the devil will continually try to find a way to cause us to stumble. He is looking for an opportune time. That's why it is important to surround ourselves with people who know these truths, who can help us especially when we are weak. I have had weeks where I am strong, and I have had weeks where I am weak. I thank God for the body of Christ who is there for me. I believe "opportune times" are those times when we are weak and vulnerable due to what life has thrown at us (e.g., a loss, a tragedy, or a bad report), and it's at these times the devil takes advantage of us the most.

The Devil Has No Legal Authority

The devil had no legal authority nor did he have entrance into Jesus, because Jesus was sinless. When we receive Christ, believing His blood was shed to remove our sin, the stamp of sin is removed from our spirit and we receive a new spirit that is just as Christ's. It is righteous, made of the same substance that is in Christ. This new heart allows us to grow in the nature and character of God. This new heart, that is righteous before God, allows us to resist the enemy. This authority to resist is not due to our merits, but in what Christ did on the cross. It is all through Him. When we make mistakes, we can ask God to forgive us, and He will, because He promised He would!6

The Disciples Walked in This Authority

We also see how Jesus gave His disciples, and then an additional 72 followers, the right to use His power to resist the devil—to drive out demons and to cure diseases while they were ministering together on the earth. At one point, the disciples returned to Jesus with reports on how the demonic influences fled from people as they prayed for them in Jesus Name.7 Jesus responded by saying, *"I saw Satan fall like lightening from heaven. I have given you authority to trample on snakes and scorpions and to overcome all the power of the enemy and nothing will harm you"* (Luke 10:18-19).

This gets me excited! Jesus, the Christ, the Master, our Savior, said those words for a reason! He knew that we would encounter seasons of our lives where we would be lambasted. He's given us clues and tools regarding our authority through Christ to say "no more" in those seasons of resistance.

Just before Jesus ascended to the Father after the resurrection He told His followers to *"Go into the entire world and preach the good news to all creation. Whoever believes and is baptized will be saved, but whoever does not believe will be condemned. And these signs will accompany those who believe: In my name they will drive out demons; they will speak in new tongues; 18 they will pick up snakes with their hands; and when they drink deadly poison, it will not hurt them at all; they will place their hands on sick people, and they will get well"* (Mark 16:15-18).

In a nutshell Jesus is saying, "In My Name, if there's something negative that's trying to come against you or preventing you from doing what I need you to do, I'm going to give you My Name to enforce My will. Things will come against you, so, I'm going to authorize you to use the authority of My Name."

I want to give you an example that has helped me to understand this concept of authority. In bygone days, a king would often send a trusted official with his own signet ring to enforce something he wanted done in that region or country. There were many reasons he might do this. For example, the king might have been implementing new taxes or laws. Whatever the reason, when the trusted delegate went to the remote region, he would show them the ring and say, "Under the authority of the king, you are ordered to do so and so." Everyone knew that if they didn't submit to what the official who was wearing the signet ring said, then an army would soon come and wreak havoc on their lives.

It is the same when we say, "In the Name of Jesus." We are not by ourselves, standing on our own authority, but there is a force behind us that is ready to back up what we have said because we are in Christ and submitted to His authority. We don't see it because it is spiritual, and we live in this natural realm, but when we say, "In Jesus' Name," we are saying, "I know what my rights and privileges are. I have been given this authority by Christ, and Christ is backing me!" Isn't that amazing?

I Was Aware of a Negative Presence

The reason why I have shared all of the above is because I was aware that there was a negative force lurking around, waiting to take advantage of my weakened state. I was aware of it. Had I not known the truth about authority failed to exercise it, I would have been like a puppet tossed all over the place. Every emotion, every imagination, would have thrown me this way and that. But I knew this stuff. I recognized that I had been weakened. I realized that I was vulnerable. And I knew that I had to make sure I stayed tight with God and tight with those who know God. I recognized the process of healing could take a lifetime or only a couple of years. (I actually ran into a woman who was still recovering 20 years later over the loss of a spouse. It doesn't need to be that way).

We Have the Holy Spirit to Resist the Enemy

Jesus provided His Holy Spirit living on the inside of us to resist and overcome the enemy. We need His authority here on earth. We won't need it in heaven, because there is no opposition in heaven, because there is no devil in heaven. You won't need your Bible. You will never need to say, "In the Name of Jesus, stop!" because the negative force won't be in heaven.

Aren't you glad that God, in His love and mercy, understood the fallen world we are living in and gave us tools in order for us to live successfully? God desires us to have a full life. When we have a full life, it's a reflection of Him. Out of that full life we can turn around and help others. There's no greater joy than when you are able to help somebody else walk in the fullness of God.

End notes:
1. Genesis 1:26-28
2. Ezekiel 28: 12-17
3. 1 Corinthians 15:45
4. 2 Corinthians 4:4
5. Luke 4:13
6. 1 John 1:9
7. Luke 9: 1-2; Luke10:1, 9, 17-19

Questions for Chapter 12:
1. Who gave Satan authority over the earth? How?

2. How are we able to resist negative things of the devil?

3. What did Jesus use to resist the devil?

4. What name can we use to resist the devil?

Reflect:
You may be experiencing the kind of gripping fear that I experienced. Realize that you have been given authority, through your relationship with Christ, over that fear. You have the right and privilege to resist negative things coming against you.

Look at Luke 10:19:
"I have given you authority to trample on snakes and scorpions and to overcome all the power of the enemy; nothing will harm you."

Act:
If you are experiencing fear say, "According to 2 Timothy 1:7, You, God, have not given me a spirit of fear but of power, love and a sound mind. God, I choose to think on good things."

Study question answers found on pages 184-190

Chapter 13: Dealing with Fear and Destructive Thoughts

I have been in the habit of conversing with God daily for years. In my healing season, I would go often to my study and simply say the Name of Jesus and cry! One morning, I was going into my study to again be in God's healing presence and as soon as I sat down in my study, I experienced something that I couldn't see come into the room and attach itself to my neck just as it had in the hospital prior to Marcus' passing away. (See chapter 12.) It was the grip of fear and grief, and I was familiar with it. I knew it existed, and I had experienced it before. I knew I had to fight it, but I was so weak. A part of me just wanted to ride the wave, to give in and let it sweep all over me. However, the Holy Spirit was gently nudging me, telling me to resist it.

I obeyed the Holy Spirit and slowly began to say, "In the Name of Jesus, stop! In the Name of Jesus, I command you to go." (Any believer can do this. You and I have been given the privilege and the honor to use the Name of Jesus as a weapon against the enemy). So, for twenty minutes I kept saying, "Lord, I know that You're faithful. I know that You love me. In the Name of Jesus, I command this evil spirit to go. I thank You right now for touching me." And then, poof! It lifted. I was fully aware that in my vulnerable condition the enemy had tried to take advantage of me.

I knew it was a spirit of grief, because I didn't just want to cry, I didn't want to live! During my healing season, believe me, I cried. Believe me, I experienced sadness. To cry and feel sad is normal, and we need to do a bit of it in order to walk through the situation and heal. The problem with crying and sadness comes when we let it completely overtake us. I mentioned in chapter 6 that grief is not just crying. Grief is where you don't even want to live.

My family was very aware of the potential for me to slip into grief, so they watched me, knowing that the enemy would try to take advantage of me. On that day I recognized the fight was on. I knew I had to be on my game because if grief tried to seize me once, I knew he'd come again. I shared in chapter 12 how the Bible says that the devil will come at an opportune time, and my time came!

Jesus Provided a Way to Resist

Now, Jesus provided a way for us to resist negative thoughts, such as feelings of giving up, grief, depression, the whole "I'm done; I can't go on" thoughts. Those are all real emotions, and it is totally normal for them to come into your head. Everyone can have them. The problem lies in what you do with them when they come. When those thoughts go unchecked (ignored, allowed to wander through our brains), our body can begin to produce toxins that hurt us. Second Corinthians 10:4-5 NKJV gives us clues about how we battle these damaging thoughts:

"For the weapons of our warfare are not carnal..." From this part of Scripture, we can see that there is warfare

going on, and we have been given weapons that are not carnal, or of this world, to fight in this warfare. We have been given something to resist the enemy. (Remember, the enemy opposes anything that is good.)

...but mighty in God for the pulling down strongholds. Our weapons are mighty, because they are through God, by our connection with God, for the purpose of pulling down strongholds in our life. *"Casting down arguments..."*

In the King James Version, *arguments* is translated "imaginations." Wow! We have weapons to cast or pull down imaginations that are negative or contrary to what God says! How many imaginations have you had to pull down today alone? False imaginations are thoughts like, "I can't." "It's impossible." or "I'm not good enough," just to name a few. All the "I cant's" and the "I'm not good enoughs" are not from God. I learned years ago that a negative thought is never from God. So, if it's not from God, I know it's from the pit of hell and it's designed to stop me. A negative thought is designed to keep me from moving forward, to keep me in a pattern of just moving side to side, looking and feeling as if I'm doing something while in reality I'm not going anywhere. *And every high thing that exalts itself against the knowledge of God.*

The knowledge of God says that we have overcome the enemy.1 The knowledge of God says that we can do all things through Christ.2 However, the imagination says, "I can't. I'm sinking. I'm done. I'm alone."

So the weapons God provides are to pull down those thoughts that say things contrary to what God would say. God says, "It doesn't matter what your situation is or how grave it appears, I can turn it around for your good."3 He is bigger than anything we will ever face in our lives!

God's Knowledge is Positive and Good

God's knowledge is positive. The devil's stuff is negative. The knowledge of God is simply what He has for you—what He wants you to do. You are vital in the earth. Don't think in any way that you are just taking up space and that you are insignificant. You are created in the image of God. You are significant. You can make a difference in your community, in your world, and the devil knows that. If the devil can keep us busy thinking that we're nothing and that we can't do anything, he wins. Let's not let him win. You are valuable because God made you. And once you become a Christ-follower, Christ is inside of you and that's why you can make such a difference in this world. Who cares what is in your past or who you used to be prior to Christ? With Him, you are a new creation.

2 Corinthians 10:4 was My Weapon

It was on the basis of the Scripture found in 2 Corinthians 10:4 that I resisted the devil when he came at me with destructive imaginations. A thought would rise in me, "Your kids are done. They're fatherless. They will never be normal, and they're going to walk with a limp. They will never be normal." And then all these statistics about fatherless girls would come to my brain. However, I became aware of what I was entertaining in my mind, and I realized that God would never say those things, so I knew those thoughts were coming from the pit of the enemy. I would say, "I cast down that imagination in the Name of Jesus. You are not from God. God's Word says that He is a father to the fatherless, a defender of widows (Isaiah 68:5), so that means that You, God, are now their father, and You are completely taking care of the girls." Had I not known the Word and its promises, and had I not used them as a weapon, I would have accepted the squirrelly thoughts. And those squirrelly thoughts would have produced toxins in my body, which would have started a destructive course for my immune system.

I heard the enemy say to me many times, "You're 35 years old, and you're a widow. You're desolate. You're done!" This is where the Lord would take me in His Word to battle that thought:

"Sing, Oh barren woman, you who never bore a child; burst into song..." (Isaiah 54:1 NIV)

I didn't feel like singing at that point.

"...Shout for joy, you who were never in labor because more are the children of the desolate women than of her who has a husband," says the LORD. "Enlarge the place of your tent, stretch your tent curtains wide, do not hold back; lengthen your cords, and strengthen your stakes. For you will spread out to the right and the left; and your descendants will dispossess nations and settle in the desolate cities. Do not be afraid; you will not suffer shame. Do not fear disgrace; you will not be humiliated. You will forget the shame of your youth and remember no more the reproach of your widowhood" (Isaiah 54:1-4).

Did this Scripture fit my circumstance or what? That's

the deliciousness of God! There are Scripture promises to meet every need we have. I'd read and declare this promise before and during a squirrelly thought.

What was I doing? I was casting down imaginations by using the tools that Jesus used and provided for us. Remember, when He spoke to the enemy, He said, "It is written."4 That is what I was doing. Many times I would speak the Word and feel nothing positive, and still I felt desolate, and I still felt like a widow. But I said it, because that's what Jesus did, and I had learned that Jesus is like my big brother and He gave me tools to use.

God Works for the Good of Those Who Love Him

And we know that in all things God works for the good of those who love him, who have been called according to his purpose (Romans 8:28).

I shared in chapter 11 that I would speak this verse and often think, "How can good come out of this! It's impossible to turn death into any good. It's so final." I couldn't see any good in this situation, but God said He works for the good of those who love him and those who are called according to His purpose.

So, I got to a point that when those squirrelly thoughts would come (telling me that my situation could never be turned around, that it's never going to go away, that no good can come of this, et cetera) the promise of God would rise up within me. Now I'm not saying that I happily jumped through my home speaking these promises and putting these Scriptures to song and dance. No, I said them out of obedience, especially when I didn't feel like it. I said them because I believed God would work on my behalf no matter what my senses said. It was a fight. And as I've learned from my mother, "Dead fish float down river. Only live ones swim up against the current."

My fight against the current, to go up stream, not to just fall prey to what was coming at me and give in to the pressure of the water, was to believe and say God's Word, despite what I was feeling. I had to keep showing up, to keep coming into His presence and say "I desperately need You, God." Because, frequently, all I wanted to do was to fall asleep and just wake up six months later with no pain and living in a new life! I just wanted the pain to stop! But every time I denied my feelings, and went into God's presence, something supernatural happened, and I always left better off than how I went in.

End notes:
1. Revelation 12:11.
2. Philippians 4:13
3. Romans 8:28
4. Matthew 4:4-10

Questions for Chapter 13:
1. According to 2 Corinthians 10:4, God gave us spiritual weapons to fight against what?

2. What is a weapon we can use to fight against destructive thoughts?

3. God's knowledge is _____; the devil's stuff is _____.

Reflect:
Have you had crazy negative imaginations bombarding you? They don't have to stick. Remember, unless you take some form of action, those crazy thoughts will govern your day and eventually have an adverse effect on you. Crazy thoughts often line up with what the world would say—not what the Word of God says.

Act:
If you are experiencing destructive thoughts say, "According to 2 Corinthians 10:45, I cast down every imagination that doesn't line up with God's Word. I refuse to have negative thoughts. Thank You, Lord, for helping me."

Study question answers found on pages 184-190

Chapter 14: Focus on God's Grace

Every one of us is going to face some form of trouble or tragedy. Trouble is a part of life because we live in a fallen world. Even Jesus said, "In this world you will have trouble."1 So, when bad things happen to us, we shouldn't be surprised, and we should not blame God. Instead, we should use the weapons He gave us to get through and not be scarred, so that we walk through to the other side of it fuller and more complete.

There is a portion of Scripture where even the Apostle Paul was sharing how he was being persecuted so much that he despaired even of life.2 He hit a point where he thought, "I don't think I can take any more." He was absolutely at his end and couldn't do anything in his own strength. He had to say, "God, I need you, and I'm desperate for you!" Paul depended on God's grace.

Grace is so big, and we really need it to live out our lives. Some of the definitions of grace are unmerited favor, moral strength or the divine assistance to perform a duty, a divine influence upon the heart. And it was God's grace, His enabling power, that delivered the Apostle Paul, and He will do the same for anyone who trusts Him! But this grace has to be received. God has extended it; we have to receive it!

Amazingly so, the Apostle Paul also wrote Philippians 4:6 *Do not be anxious about anything, but in everything, by prayer and petition, with thanksgiving, present your requests to God.* This verse shows us that there is a potential for anxiety and fear to come.

Let's go back to the encounter I had in my study with the spirit of fear and grief (see chapter 13). I was on my way to talk to the Lord, and anxiety came. And how do we battle anxiety? We can't simply think it away. We have to say something. I was battling, so I knew I had to pray, just as Philippians 4:6 tells us. Look again what it says here, "...But in everything by prayer and petition, with thanksgiving..." (Prayer is simply talking to God, using our voice, presenting to Him specifically what our concern is).

So, the anxiety came, the fear came, and I had to use some words to make my request to God. I had to say, "In Jesus' Name, anxiety go!" (Because it is clear in the Scriptures that it is by the Name of Jesus that we have access to ask God for things.) Paul continues in Philippians 4:7, *And the peace of God, which transcends all understanding, will guard your hearts and minds in Christ Jesus.*

I don't know how it happens. All I know is that within 20 minutes this peace came in and it truly transcended my understanding! It's a spiritual thing. How do you explain spiritual things? Many of the things of God aren't meant to be put in words, because our words can't begin to describe His enormity, His perfection—they are meant to be experienced. I just know it happened.

There was a time when I didn't understand how peace could be that big, but now I have experienced it. It is God-big. Words can't explain it. We all should strive to know that peace. I declared this verse (Philippians 4:7),

The peace of God that transcends all understanding is guarding my heart and mind in the name of Jesus. As I said it, let me tell you I was shaking, I had tears running down my face, but indeed that peace that transcends all understanding, came and wiped away the anxiety.

Focus on the Good

If we continue with Philippians 4:8 we read, *Finally brothers, whatever is true, whatever is noble, whatever is right, whatever is pure, whatever is lovely, whatever is admirable—if anything is excellent or praise worthy— think about such things.* In earlier chapters, I started off by saying that we have to create an environment for healing on purpose (see chapters 6-11). Well, on purpose, I had to think on lovely things. What does that mean? When a thought would arise about how bad the situation was, on purpose I had to focus on the good in my life: "I have three healthy children. I have a family that loves me. I have a roof over my head." If we don't look at the positives in our lives we will drown in the negative.

I never allowed my kids to see me break down (I only broke down with my mom), because their eyes were on me for reassurance that they were going to be okay, that we were going to make it through this. And when they would say, "Mommy, it's so bad, it hurts so much!" I had to say, "I know, but you have me. We have our house, we have our family, we have your grandparents." I had to put their minds constantly on good things, because they couldn't do it for themselves.

If we have children who have experienced a loss, it's up to us as parents to put those mental images in their little brains. We have to let them know that there's still life after the loss—there's still good in their lives. Otherwise, by default they will focus just on the loss and can drown in that emotion of loss.

My mother helped me to not look at the issues at hand. She would say, "God has a plan for your life. He's not done with you, girl. You have a lot of life in you still." I needed to hear that because I didn't feel like I had life in me. We all need that, don't we? That's why it's so important not to go through this alone. We need to be connected on purpose with the body of Jesus Christ.

Negative Thoughts Come Easily

It's so easy to focus on all the bad things, like, "I can't pay my bills," or "I hate my job," et cetera. It's a lot harder to think on what is working in our lives. Thinking on those things that are working in our lives gives us the energy and strength to endure our current situations as we wait for those changes to come that we so desire. If we focus on the negative, we don't even have the energy or the strength to deal with the issues at hand.

There's a Fight for Healing

I want to encourage you by making it clear that there is a fight at times to receive healing. We want healing, and we want it now! But we have to go to the Healer and cooperate with His ways. Cooperating with Him isn't a step that is accomplished overnight. It is a process that we walk through over a period of time. Those who know me well are very familiar with my saying, "It's a process." And when they finish telling me their situation so I can counsel with them, they almost stop me as I speak and finish my statement for me. "I know, it's a process." I smile at them and nod. Life is a process!

Through God, we can receive healing, and even though it takes time, it is still faster and is more complete than any healing the world's system can offer. We live in a world of instant messaging and drive-through windows, where things happen so fast. It can be a challenge for us to accept the process, but God is faithful and will give us all sorts of yummy tidbits while we journey with Him. Our process will be a journey in which we get to gather all sorts of treasures as we head toward our destination.

During this process of my healing, the false imaginations were often huge and oppressive. It was something I battled every single day, and my family was fully aware of it. They would walk by me and say, "You have a glorious future. I don't care what it looks like. You have a glorious future." By saying those encouraging Bible promises, they caused me to focus on the good. Those Bible promises spoken to me brought healing to my soul.

Every time we speak the Word of God, it's as if there's a tap into our soul. Imagine our soul as a cup, and every time we speak the healing Word of God, we're adding more substance to that cup. We're filling it to the point where eventually it spills over and erases all of the negative stuff.

My family continued to speak encouraging promises to me. I couldn't have done it by myself. I don't know how people do it by themselves. We weren't meant to do this by ourselves. I was surrounded. They couldn't do all the fighting for me, and I couldn't do it all by myself. We had to cooperate. That's what the body of Christ was designed to do.

Weapons will Form

Isaiah 54:17 NKJV says that "no weapon formed against you shall prosper." This is true when we know how to use God's Word. However, the weapons will come and prosper if we don't do something—if we don't use His Word. Imagine a burglar coming to your house and you have a gun, but you don't know how to use it, and the burglar takes the gun from you and then uses it on you. Wouldn't that be horrible? Well, that's a weapon being formed against you. But when we know how to use God's Word, and we implement what we know, those weapons of the enemy can't be used against us, and thus, they cannot prosper.

If you don't know how to access the Word of God, find a church where the Word is taught and get into a small group. Get with somebody who can help you. I needed help to learn how to do that. We all need help to learn how to access these promises that Jesus provided for us, and once we know about them, we still need people to help us stand on the Word. Are you getting the message that we need people to walk through life with?

End notes:
1. John 16:33
2. 2 Corinthians 1:8

Questions for Chapter 14:
1. What does grace mean?

2. How do we get grace?

3. When a negative thought arises in our thinking, what should we focus on?

4. What does Philippians 4:8 say we should do?

Reflect:
In the midst of the tragedy/crisis, has it been a struggle to think on the good things in your life?

Act:
On purpose think on the things you are grateful for. Say, "According to Philippians 4:8, I will think on things that are true, noble, right, pure, lovely, and admirable."

Study question answers found on pages 184-190

Live Again

A true story of overcoming los

Chapter 15: Clarity

"Ask and it will be given to you; seek and you will find; knock and the door will be opened to you."
— Matthew 7:7

In Matthew 7:7, Jesus is telling us that if we need some answers and we pursue God for those answers, He will give them to us. Now I'm not saying every single answer in the cosmos is available to us. No, there are mysteries that will be kept until we see Christ face to face. I have some questions that I am going to ask Him when I see Him face to face. For example, I'm going to ask about the mystery of why we ladies have to carry the babies, and why it takes longer for women's bodies to get into shape than men's!

Everyone Seeks Closure

Everyone seeks closure when they go through some form of a loss. Whether it's a divorce, loss of a spouse, a child, a dream, any kind of loss, our whole being desires closure. We want to be able to file it somewhere; to make sense of it and then move on. Our soul longs for that kind of closure.

On the day of Marcus' homegoing service I had the pleasure of being with Bishop Keith Butler. He performed the service, and he really was a catalyst in my personal healing. While we were together that day, he told me that within ninety days I would have clarity. Now at the time, I really did not understand what he meant by that. I just knew that I needed to make it through the funeral. The funeral was all I could think about. But the process of clarity began almost immediately.

When I say clarity, I mean the "Why, God, why?" of it all. I'm not saying that I am ever going to understand fully all of the "whys," but I trust God that He will fill me in on what I need to know. The responsibility of knowing all the "whys" seems almost too big anyway. Even this past week, while preparing this material, I received a greater understanding about Marcus. So, I believe my clarity is still in a process, but I believe the bulk of it came within those first ninety days, just as Bishop Butler had said.

Dreams Can Bring Clarity

God will use dreams to speak to us. We can see this throughout the Bible, both in the Old and the New Testaments. We can recall the story of Mary and Joseph. Joseph was just about to divorce Mary, because she had told him that she was pregnant with the Seed of God by the Holy Spirit. And I can just imagine what Joseph thought when he heard that the first time, "Okay, Mary what are you on?" But God revealed through a dream to Joseph that what Mary had said was true. God came to her defense through a dream.

There are all kinds of times in the Bible where a dream was given to warn of an impending danger. And God still uses dreams today. Revelation dreams have been experienced in our family quite a bit, and many of them have given us warnings of demonic plans against our family. God is so merciful. He is so kind.

What I have found, many times, is that God is speaking to me, but I'm too busy in my thinking to hear Him. Sometimes, when I'm so preoccupied with life, He speaks to me through dreams, because I can't do anything but hear when I sleep. The day after Marcus passed I had a recurring dream all night. This recurring dream was the beginning of my personal clarity.

In the dream, Marcus was at the hospital and I was there, speaking healing promises from the Bible over his physical body. I was saying, "The same Spirit that raised Christ from the dead dwells in you and quickens your body. I say your body is being quickened by the Spirit of God." This Scripture is from Romans 8:11. That was the main Scripture that I was saying in the dream, and whenever I said it in the dream, he would revive. I was so exhausted in the dream that I left the hospital to go home and rest. As soon as I would get home the phone would ring and it would be the nurse saying, "Mrs. Stefano, Mrs. Stefano, we're losing him, you need to come again!" In the dream, I would return to the hospital, speaking the Word over Marcus again until he would revive. Once he revived, I would go home.

This dream happened all night, and I knew the Lord was trying to show me that the Word of God does work. You see, many times when there is a death we begin to question, "Does God really heal?" "Does His Word always work?" Through this dream, God, in His mercy, was showing me that the times I spoke the Word over Marcus' body, he was revived.

Speaking God's Word Does Work

Many times during the two years of fighting cancer, I spoke God's healing Word over Marcus and received results. One time, when Marcus was still alive, we had to go to the hospital because a medical treatment caused his white blood count to drop so low that he was unable to fight off any bacteria or virus. The doctors told me that he would probably be there for at least three to four weeks recovering, and that usually meant that I was with him and not with my kids. After the doctors left, I lay partially on Marcus and began to speak the Word of God over his body. I began to say, "In the Name of Jesus Christ, you white blood cells, you need to multiply right now. I'm not going to stay in this hospital for four weeks. I have babies to raise." I prayed for awhile, thinking for sure that in the morning I would get a great report. However, in the morning they told me it was worse. Has anyone ever been there?

I said, "It doesn't matter what it looks like, I'm going to continue to stand on the Word because I need to get home." To make a long story short, by the next day the white blood cells were completely up. The doctor came in absolutely dumbfounded. He said he didn't know how this happened, and he released Marcus to go home. I saw this constantly in the process of Marcus' battle against cancer—the Word of God working.

Whenever Marcus would feel a symptom, there was a tendency for him to go into fear. How many of you are tempted to fear when you feel a symptom? It's very normal. Throughout our married life, Marcus was rarely sick. He was always very healthy. I was the one who had many limitations in my physical body. So when I found out about the Scriptural promises regarding healing that were available for us as Christ-followers, I desperately began to apply them to the limitations in my body. In my personal walk with God, I began to apply God's healing Word over my body one area at a time, and I got great results.

In the Old Testament we see that God delivered His special people, the Israelites, from the oppression of the Egyptians. They were supposed to journey through the desert and end up in this remarkable land, all of which would be theirs forever. Deuteronomy 7:22 shows us that the Lord told Joshua, their leader, that He would give the Israelites the land a little at a time, not all at once. That is how it was with my physical body—it was the land I had to conquer one part at a time.

And it's the promises of God that afforded me this wonderful opportunity! I began to apply the principles of the Word of God to each area of my physical body and, one at a time, each area began to line up with the Word. I was even healed of an incurable sickness.

It Has to be Personal

When Marcus was diagnosed with cancer, because of my personal experiences with the Word of God, I believed we would overcome. I have since then found that my personal experience with God's Word may help others a little, but eventually everyone has to have a personal experience with the Word of God if it is going to sustain each person's own life. For many of the physical problems I had, there were no remedies or cures, so I was forced to depend on the Word of God for healing. It was my only choice. I'm so glad that I learned how to depend on the Word, because now I'm not afraid when something comes at me. I know that God's Word can change any situation. You see, the Bible is just a book with words in it, ineffective, inoperative, until some-body says, "I believe that it's for me" and then begins to speak what it says. It's like taking medicine from a cabinet, putting it in your hand and then putting it in your mouth. That medicine in that cabinet is ineffective until somebody opens up that vile and puts it in his/her mouth.

The Word is Medicine

Recently, I was sitting in a church service on a Wednes-day night, and I began to feel shivers all over my body. By Friday, upon going to the doctor, I was diagnosed with severe influenza. I was told I would be on my back for two weeks, but I was scheduled to teach on Sunday! I couldn't be on my back for two weeks! So I took Prov-erbs 4:20-22 NKJV as medicine to my body:

My son pay attention to my words, incline your ear to my sayings. Do not let them depart from your eyes...

Notice it is says, "Give attention to my Word." Have you ever been in a class and your mind traveled all over the place instead of listening to the instructor? But then all of a sudden the instructor says there is going to be a pop quiz at the end of the lecture. What happens to your at-tention? Now you are listening, because you know you need to keep that information to do something with it.

My son, pay attention to my words, incline your ear to my sayings. Do not let them depart from your eyes... These Scripture verses reference our minds, eyes, and ears; meaning that our whole being is involved.

The Scripture continues, *...Keep them in the midst of*

your heart; for they are life to those who find them and health to all their flesh. This is what is interesting, that word *flesh* actually, literally means *"flesh"*—not spiritual flesh, but natural flesh—our bodies. You can't spiritualize this particular Scripture. It actually means flesh, blood, and bones. This Word, God says, is health to all of our flesh.

What God is trying to get over to us is, "By faith can you believe that when you say this Scripture, this promise, that medicine is actually going into your body?" Yes, I can do that! But it doesn't make sense, does it? "You mean as I say this Word, something is going into my physical body?" Yes! I didn't say it. God did. It takes somebody to believe it. When somebody believes the Word, now it becomes operative and effective.

So that particular Scripture was my medicine, my "antibiotic," when I was diagnosed with severe influenza. I was so tired I could barely speak. My body was so tired. However, even though it felt like my head and my body were not connected, I kept saying that particular Scripture. I kept saying, "Lord, my body is getting stronger by the second (cough, gag)." It was a fight. On Sunday morning, up until I took the pulpit, my legs were shaking, my chest had a tickle, and I still was saying, "God, help!" But the minute I stood up, God's presence—His power—showed up on me in a way I can't even describe.

Again I ask, how can you describe spiritual things with mere words? I still can't wrap my brain around it. I just believe it because He said it. I try my best to explain it to people, but I can't explain certain things because they are spiritually appraised. It came on me in such power.

I was so aware that the Spirit of God loved the people so much that He was willing to use anything that stood behind that pulpit. It was almost as if I were watching myself teach. It was kind of fun. I'm so grateful for the numerous teachings I've received instructing me, as a Christ-follower, that the Word of God can have a medicinal effect to my physical body.

By Christ's Wounds We are Healed

In Isaiah 53:3 NKJV we read, *He was despised and rejected by men....* Isaiah was talking about Jesus Christ. He was prophesying about what Christ would do years in the future. *...A Man of sorrows and acquainted with grief.... Sorrows* here is pain, and *grief* is sickness. That is the actual, literal translation.

...And we hid, as if it were, our faces from Him. He was despised, and we did not esteem Him. Surely He has borne our griefs (sickness) and carried our sorrows (pains); yet we esteemed Him stricken, smitten by God, and afflicted. But He was wounded for our transgressions; He was bruised for our iniquities...

"*Transgressions*" is translated as when we cross over a boundary line and we say, "Oh, I just transgressed. I just crossed over that boundary line." Well, Jesus was bruised for that, but He was also crushed for our iniquities. An iniquity is when a person habitually transgresses until the wrongdoing has become a part of who they are. They've become completely desensitized to the wrongdoing. (I'm so glad that He took care of it all at the cross, and He didn't leave anything out.)

...And by His stripes we are healed. Christ received stripes, an awful, terrible whipping, on His back prior

to going to the cross. He received those stripes so we could be healed. It doesn't say that we are going to be healed sometime in the future. It says that we are healed!

Most of the time when we talk about Christ, it is in reference to salvation, meaning we are saved from our sins. As we've read in earlier chapters, when sin came into the earth, sickness came with it. Sickness is one of the effects or by-products of sin.We can conclude, then, that if you deal with the root problem of sin, you can deal with the fruit of sickness. Correct? No sin—no sickness. That is just how it is. Jesus dealt with sickness. His body was bruised, and His body was broken, so that we would have an opportunity to resist sickness when it comes against us. We cannot separate salvation and healing—they are one. Healing is a part of our salvation. This was a deep truth for me.

When Breakthrough Doesn't Seem to Come

I've prayed many times and didn't have a breakthrough. I didn't say, "Well, the Word doesn't work," because I recognized my human fallibility. I recognize that I, as a human being, can err. I'm not always on my game... that I can miss it. I'm not going to judge the Creator of the entire world based on my experience alone—the human experience that can change like the wind. His Word is true and consistent in my life. When it seems that it's not, either I have to make some adjustments or else I'm in a process, and I'm not ready for some things. My point is that I recognize my human-ness. I recognize that I'm in a process of growing and becoming like Him. I recognize that I'm not going to "arrive" until I see Him face-to-face. So that means that there's going to be potential for new revelation, for new understanding, and for missing it. Why? Because we are human.

This has been a major foundation for me personally. There have been times when I have prayed over my kids, and literally, fevers would just leave them. Then there are other times when they had to go through a healing process. I don't understand all the "whys" of the process, but what I do know is that the Word works, and if it's not working, I'm not going to question God about it. We hate to look at ourselves from a "not-there-yet-still-growing" perspective. I'm so settled that until I see Him face-to-face that I will be growing. I'm so settled that I'm going to make mistakes every day, and I'm okay with that. I don't martyr myself as I used to.

I was the best martyr. I would make a mistake and begin saying, "Oh my God, how could I?" Well, I am human, that's why. It's a waste of time to martyr ourselves. It's a waste of time because God is not in it. He is into forgiveness. God is into getting us back on track. The devil is into having us crucify ourselves and make us feel as low as worms. God never does that.

Healing was a Part of Me

Anything that had to do with healing was so a part of me because I had personally been healed of so many things. When the onslaught of cancer came on Marcus, I had a "no defeat, no losing the battle" mindset. I was a living, breathing example of this Word bringing healing to all my flesh.

There was a man sitting in one of our church services listening to me teach on healing, and he said, referring to me, "I won't even try to debate with her, because she is so convinced." Why am I so convinced? Because I have had a personal encounter with the Word regarding healing. I am breathing because of the Word of healing. My daughter, Taressa, has legs because of the Word of healing. Alexa is alive because of the Word of healing. Daniela swallowed the meconium while I was giving birth to her, and she could have died. Thank God for His healing Word!

So when it came to Marcus, I was absolutely set; standing firm, thinking, of course, he was going to be healed. I even had a dream a few days before he passed that he did die, but I refused to believe it. Obviously God was trying to get a hold of me to let go, to prepare, but I couldn't hear that. And in the dream, I was crying hysterically because he had passed. I got up out of that dream, saying, "In the name of Jesus, NOOO!!!" We have a hard time letting go of loved ones.

It's about Your Own Personal Faith

Another recurring flashback helped bring clarity regarding the passing of Marcus. I kept revisiting a particular moment when Marcus and I were watching a great preacher talk about the authority and power we have in the Word of God. Marcus was in the middle of his fight with cancer. The preacher gave an example of his wife who had gotten sick and she had to go in for surgery. However, the surgery was very risky. The Lord said to this preacher, "Every time your wife has come down with something, you have prayed for her and she went on your coat tails. I want her to use the Word for herself this time." Well, the doctors had told his wife she may or may not make it through the surgery they were planning to do, so the preacher asked her what she could believe for. She believed that God would heal her through the surgery—that's where her faith was. Her husband, on the other hand, had enough faith to believe that she didn't need the surgery. It wasn't about his faith this time, but rather hers. It was time for her to walk.

We do the same with our children. When we teach our children to walk and they decide they don't want to, do we say, "Okay, I'll carry you forever?" No. And when they fall do we say, "You poor thing, you can't walk?" No. We say, "Get back up and try again. Come on, keep going. You can do it!" There comes a time when we have to say "walk!"

By the way, the preacher's wife ended up going through the surgery and outliving that preacher! While we were watching this great preacher talk, Marcus looked at me and said, "Tracy, it's not going to be your faith this time. It's my deal. This is between God and me." I got so afraid when he said that. I knew that I had multiple experiences with the Word of God that he hadn't. My mother and I spent hours speaking over his physical body when he would sleep, and we would see changes in his physical body, but there came a point where it was between him and God, as he said.

Another Dream...Further Clarity

When Marcus had passed away in the hospital, I was very upset that he left. I stayed with him for five hours and spoke to his body and told him that he couldn't leave me by myself. Finally, the nurses said that I needed to sign the papers and move on.

Three nights after he passed, I had a dream that brought further clarity. This dream was almost humorous, for I was hitting Marcus! (And that's just not like me.) In my dream, Marcus came back from heaven apparently at my request, but he would not look at me. He kept his eyes upward, looking to heaven as if he were looking at God. I knew he did not want to be with me and that he wanted to go back to heaven. The look he had in his eyes said, "I let her see me, now can I come back?" I was so upset at him that I began hitting him and screaming at him saying that he had to stay with me...that I needed him more than heaven did!

When I woke up from that dream, I understood that he had an opportunity to come back, but he did not want to be here.

Clarity Helped Bring Closure

People wondered how I healed so well, and in a fairly decent amount of time. I'll tell you, it is because my God is so merciful, so kind, and so tender. He began to bring clarity to me. I asked for this clarity, and He began to put the pieces together to help me understand.

I'm not saying it was all hunky-dory during that time. There was one day, even with all that I know about the Word of God, and all that He was speaking to me, that I stood up and was having a moment. (Have you ever had a moment? Have you ever had a pity party?) I stood up and looked out the window and cried, "What exit did I get off at? Why?" I knew the "whys," but it felt good to ask it. I wanted the pain to leave yesterday, but it was a process. And a part of the healing was clarity. It brought closure in my thoughts.

Live Again

A true story of overcoming los

Questions for Chapter 15:
1. What was one of the venues that brought clarity to me?

2. What is "health" to all our flesh (Proverbs 4:20-22)?

3. What does the word "sorrow" mean in Isaiah 53: 3-4?

Reflect:
Do you find your mind racing, seeking answers? Do the thoughts you have even seem painful? Jesus carried the pain that you are experiencing right now. Allow Him to touch you. Allow Him to remove the pain.

Act:
Read Matthew 7:7, "Ask and it will be given, seek and you will find, knock and the door will be opened." Ask God to give you further clarity. Expect answers!

Study question answers found on pages 184-190

Live Again

A true story of overcoming los

Chapter 16: Thoughts Matter

Our Thought Life Can Heal or Bring on Disease

So many speculate the origins of sickness—how it has access to us. As we stated before, much sickness is directly related to our thought life. This is such powerful knowledge, it is worthy of discussing again, and again, and again. *For the Word of God is living and it's active* (Hebrews 4:12).

The words *living* and *active* mean "powerful to do something, to bring change!" This Word not only produces healing, but transforms our thought processes as well. The more our thoughts are saturated with the healing Word the more healing can come.

I wrote in chapter 4 that much of the disease today can be linked back to our thought life. If our thoughts are full of fear, past abuses, anxiety, or stress, how are we going to make it? How many times have we heard, "Oh, he was 54 and suddenly died of a heart attack?" It all seems sudden to us because we don't see the person's choices accumulate over time into something that results in an illness. A healthy heart just doesn't stop beating one day with no cause. And stress can be one of these causes.

Stressful thoughts over a long period of time can break down the body. If a person, full of stress, comes to me for prayer for a physical ailment caused by stress, they may experience a temporary release of pain, much like taking an anti-inflammatory or something. If the environment producing the stress does not change, however, the physical body will again experience a physical problem. If the thought process producing stress does not change, toxins will continue to be released in the body, causing sickness. A lot of pain relievers do not cure or heal. They only mask the problem and give temporary relief. If we don't deal with the root of the sickness, it won't go away.

There were many things I understood about Marcus' passing over the years, but this was huge for me. Marcus had stressful thoughts because he had been abused as a young boy, and even in his early teens. There were certain things about his upbringing, about the environments that he was in, that shaped who he was.

I can't imagine what it is to live with that. I've never been abused, but I've counseled many people who have, and it's still hard to understand. Similarly, it's difficult for people to be able to truly understand what the loss of a loved one is like unless they have gone through it. You can identify, but to really understand is impossible.

I don't know the ghosts that Marcus dealt with or the things that he didn't want to look at, but I believe that there was stuff there. I've learned over the years, when one has been abused there is a ton of self-loathing as well as a sense of unworthiness to receive God's grace.

As I had mentioned earlier in the book, I had walked into Marcus' hospital room a few days before he passed and didn't say a word. I didn't say hello, nothing. I simply looked at him and right up out of my heart came these words, "You are forgiven." He looked at me as if he had never heard those words before, and he was a Pastor. I knew then that we were in trouble. You can't have faith and fear in the same place. I saw awe in his face. Although I was married to him, I never knew there was something he couldn't forgive about himself. I asked him, "Do you realize how great you are? Do you know what a great person you are?" He couldn't receive those words from me.

We don't understand the psyche of other people. We don't understand their thought patterns. We don't understand where they've come from, the hurt they have experienced, or the pain that they have walked through. And a lot of that, believe it or not, affects the physical body, because as I mentioned before, ailments in our physical bodies many times are a result of how and what we think. That's why God frequently says in the Bible that we need to pay attention to our thoughts: *Be transformed by the renewing of your mind with the Word of God* (Romans 12:2).

That word *transformed* means "metamorphosis,"[1] like going from being a caterpillar to a butterfly. Why did God say that? Because He understood that we all come to Christ with a past, which includes many issues! Often, we didn't even cause a lot of those issues. We were in environments that shaped us. The way to change our thought processes and clean out yuck in our heads is by using the Word of God.

When we read God's Word, it supernaturally cleans our minds. It gets rid of the junk and fills our minds with His good Words for us. After time in His Word, all of a sudden we are no longer thinking fear and unforgiveness and "I'm not good; I'm not adequate." Instead we begin to think, "I am loved. I am righteous." We don't wake up feeling righteous; we don't. We usually wake up thinking, "Oh my God, I've got to face this person that I just yelled at and I have to call that person I offended and ask them to forgive me." That is why every day I love that I can say, "Thank You, God, that I'm forgiven. I'm starting fresh today."

We don't know what races through people's minds and thought life. We don't know if people's thoughts are filled with fear or faith. We can't judge them because we don't live in their brains. It doesn't make them bad people. If a person has a hard time forgiving themselves, or can't forget the pain they caused people, it will eat them up inside. Have you ever met people like that, who just can't forgive themselves? We may not understand where people are. It doesn't make them bad people; it means they are human.

There are limitations at times when it comes to healing, and we shouldn't judge people when they don't receive their healing right away, or when they don't see their healing until they go home to be with the Lord. Instead, it'd be better for us to recognize that we don't understand their thought processes. We can't see into the depths of their being. I have a hard time with my own thoughts, let alone someone else's thoughts. But let's not question the Word of God based on a human experience. God heals!

I knew it wasn't God's best for Marcus to leave this earth so young. I recognized that we're all human, and that really was another big key to my personal healing; I understood my humanness! That is why I didn't have to go to God with, "I just don't understand." I really believe that had I not had the foundation of God's Word, the environment of my church (Life Christian Church), and strong believers in God's Word around me, I would have gone the same way everyone else did, questioning God. I would have, hands down. What happened instead was that the Word I had studied, or placed in my heart, would rise up in me and come out of my mouth. Even when I lay my head down on my pillow, the Word would come right up to my brain confirming His love for me, His plans for me and His character.

In the middle of a crisis, we see if we have the Word in us, for we will either respond with the Word or with a negative emotion. There have been times that I recognized that I didn't have enough Word in me in a crisis. Has anyone else been there? Instead of responding with a positive, loving, God-like answer, I was short, brash or irritable, proving I needed more of God's changing Word in me.

Create Your Own Environment of the Word

Transformed-thinking eliminates a bulk of junk that otherwise gets into our physical bodies. It's so important to have a consistency in the Word, so that when we go through something like a loss, for example, we won't be open for potential sickness due to the overwhelming grief that we experience. Start today to make a commitment to create environments where you are hearing the Word of God; whether it's a small group, a church environment, or a private environment. We need to create that environment for ourselves. No one will do it for us.

I can guarantee you will be able to come up with many

excuses as to why you don't have time, but it is something we all need to make a priority. The Word in us produces a powerful existence. We don't know when the day of trouble is coming. If we knew, we would do something about it. If every day we spend some time in the Word of God, beginning with a little bit of time, then adding a little bit more, and a little bit more, then we come to see that God is actually preparing us on the inside to face any calamity that is coming down the road.

Life is calamity. Haven't we figured that out yet? Life is filled with calamities, and God's Word becomes a garrison, a strength to face what we need to face. Just as eating spinach or taking vitamins builds up our bodies, so the Word of God works when trouble comes, and we are not floored.

Have you ever seen those punching bags that when you knock them down come back up? We, like those punching bags, can keep coming back up, because the Word of God is sustaining us. You can't knock a Christian down and keep him down. Though the righteous may fall seven times, the Word says, he always rises again.2

Sickness Is in the Air

There are many reasons for sickness, including a person's diet, heredity factors, or stress. Disease and sickness are in the air because we live in a fallen world. There is a lot of stuff flying around in the air ready to land on us. One day, when I was struggling in my physical body, I happened to open up a book and on this particular page it said that when we experience stress in our physical bodies, our cellular function breaks down, and that is how we "catch" the cold or flu.3

I remember years ago when I was in college, I had stayed up all night doing something (I was just beginning to learn these things and was putting some of them into practice), and I walked outside of my dormitory into the cold brisk air heading toward the gym for cheerleading practice. Immediately, I could feel something come on my throat like the common cold. It was if I had walked right into that virus. It was in the air, and I walked into it, and my body was already weakened from having stayed up all night. I remember saying, "God, forgive me for pulling an all-nighter. God, I ask You right now to touch me." Right then and there, when I was fully aware of it and on my walk to the gym (which was about a quarter mile away), I kept saying, "In the Name of Jesus, thank You for healing me. Thank You for touching me right now." By the time I got to the gym it had completely lifted from me.

I had run into that virus. It was in the air. We live in a fallen world that is filled with stuff that we will run into. Had I not known the Word of God, I could not have dealt with that common cold that way, could I? But I was aware. Now, I'm not saying I'm always aware. There are times when it goes right over my head, because I'm too busy or distracted. Instead of slowing down, I pop some vitamins in my mouth and keep going. Eventually, it catches up with me and I find myself flat on my back. However, when I catch it and I'm on my game, it doesn't run its course in me.

Why Do Bad Things Happen?

People have often asked me why babies die right out of the womb. Without hesitation I tell them it's the product of a fallen world. If we don't know that we can do something about a bad report, then we simply take what comes our way. All three of my babies had something come against them in my womb. Had I not known these truths, they would not be where they are today. I know, that I know, that I know.

But why do these negative things happen? Because we live in a fallen world with a sick ruler, and you can't figure out his plan and why he does what he does. He is sick. He is the author of a lot of the junk that is happening in this fallen world we live in. I've heard people say, "Well, God allowed it." God allows everything because He has to. He allows the world to continue as it is, because He has to. It is on a particular lease, and when Christ returns and there is a renewal of all things, it doesn't have to be that way anymore. But until He does return, God is limited to our free will and our choices. Just as I said a few chapters ago, you can go out and eat as much chocolate cake as you want and no one will stop you. You can run up your credit card bill and no one will stop you. God has given us a free will to choose His ways or our ways. And our ways, many times, are manipulated by something outside of ourselves and outside of God.

Lifestyle Affects Our Health

Now I'm not saying that when it comes to sickness that it is only in the air. Sometimes it is just a lifestyle change we need to make. I know that in September of 2004, I was sick for a whole month. I could not get well. I remember my new husband James saying, "What is wrong with you?" I told him that I'd tell him if I knew. So I began to talk to God about what was going on. Basically, I discovered that I had to make a couple of adjustments in my diet, and I began to do it consistently. Just as I take vitamins every day, I began to take a few healing Scriptures every day for maintenance. We have vitamins for maintenance of physical bodies, and we have Scriptural promises for maintenance on our physical bodies. It is a blend of the natural and the supernatural. So I made a couple of adjustments, nothing major, and I have experienced great health ever since.

Mysteries We'll Never Know

As we've already read, there are some mysteries to which we will never have answers. We can't figure God out in every single instance and in every single situation that happens. I don't want anyone reading this to think that we can know everything—we can't. Because if we could know everything, then that would mean that God is very small. And we know that He's not. There are certain things we can know. Yet there are certain things, that if we ask the Lord for clarity on, He will bring it to us.

I don't think I'm special. I don't think God said, "I'm just going to favor you, Tracy, with this information." No. I don't believe that. God is not a respecter of persons. He loves all of us. I just sought it out. I asked those questions, and I got the answers that I needed, and I'm still in a process of getting answers.

We Are the Keeper of Our Thoughts

I have a very clear, healthy mind. I sleep very well at night, and I know it's the product of the teachings I've received and my associations—people who build me up and encourage me. I watch my observations—what goes in my eye-gate and in my ear-gate. I'm the type of per-

person who can't sit through a violent movie; I just can't handle it. (Some people can handle it—I can't.) I'm a very visual person and I'll replay all that in my mind. If it has a bad ending, I can't resolve it. I have a hard time with that, so I don't do that to myself anymore, because I am the keeper of my physical body.

I'm going to revisit this Scripture again in Proverbs 4:20-23, which reveals that we are responsible to keep our hearts and minds right. It's nobody else's responsibility:

My son, pay attention to what I say; listen closely to my words. Do not let them out of your sight; keep them within your heart; for they are life to those who find them and health to a man's whole body. Above all else, guard your heart, for it is the wellspring of life.

Again, we have to be careful where our minds go. I'm very careful with my thoughts. If I'm having a negative thought about myself, I stop. I'll say out loud, "No! God would not say that, and I'm not going to say that about myself." Or if I'm thinking that a person is not going to pull off what he said he would do, I'll stop myself from judging him. Have you had a negatively thought about somebody?

When I start thinking something negatively about somebody, I call myself on the carpet. I'd rather call myself on the carpet than let that thing run rampant in my brain and begin to produce something that I don't want in my physical body. That is why the Word said to think on those things that are pure, lovely and of good report.4 Why? It's for our own health...for our own well-being. It's not for anybody else's, but for our own well-being.

We have to monitor what we are allowing in our minds and in our thought life. What are our observations? And, we need to ask ourselves: Are there some relationships that we need to limit a little because they are not building us up, but instead they are tearing us down? Have we listened to some teachings that are causing us to doubt the awesomeness and graciousness of our God? We need to do our own check. A healthy mind produces a healthy body.

End Notes:
1. PC Study Bible: Strong's Greek/Hebrew Dictionary
2. Proverbs 24:16
3. Leaf, Dr. Caroline,—Who Switched Off My Brain?—Page 40, South Africa: Switch on Your Brain Organisation PTY, 2007. Print.
4. Philippians 4:8

Questions for Chapter 16
1. In Hebrews 4:12, what does the word "living" and "active" mean?

2. The Word not only produces _____ but transforms our _____ process.

3. Why do seemingly innocent have bad things happen to them?

4. Who is responsible to keep our heart and mind right?

Reflect:
Where have your thoughts been? Have they been stressful? Do you feel you have been physically affected by your thought process?

Act:
On purpose begin to transform any negative thoughts to positive thoughts. As you are about to read the Bible, say, "Father, in Jesus name, I believe you are transforming my thoughts as I read your Word and purpose to apply it. I believed I am loved, and I am righteous because I am yours."

Study question answers found on pages 184-190

Chapter 17: Get Busy

The healing we desire is a process. The daily times in my devotions were opportunities for healing. I have often told people to simply "show up." Just show up in the presence of God. Show up in some kind of appointment or time with God. Open up your Bible and trust that where ever you read, whether you choose something from the New Testament or Proverbs, trust that God is going to speak. The Bible is as a love letter. I fell in love with James (my new husband) through emails. Although he wasn't there when I read them, this amazing thing happens when you read a letter from someone you love. There is something that is transferred to you. It is the same way with the Bible. Every time you open up the Word of God, trust that God is preparing you for whatever it is you need...and that He's healing your heart. That is simply the process. That daily time I spent with Him allowed that healing to come.

I was aware of the healing process that was going on as I continued practicing the things I have written about. After about three months, something happened that showed me what God was doing to my soul. One evening I was home by myself (which was extremely rare for me). I decided to go on my computer and start cleaning up my desktop because there was so much junk on it. I happened to click one icon when all of a sudden this video image of Marcus came on the screen with him talking. Apparently, at some point, he had purchased some new equipment and was experimenting with it and never erased it. I hadn't seen him for three months, not in a picture...nothing...and suddenly, he pops up talking and laughing on my computer. I just froze. I kept playing it over and over. It would stop, and I would play it again. As I continued to press the icon over and over, I was evaluating where I was in my healing. I was in awe because I was aware that some healing had happened in me. I didn't go crazy, I didn't fall apart, I didn't lose it when I saw his handsome face and heard his laugh. I was fine. I was hurting some, but I was fine. I said, "Oh my God, God you are carrying me, I'm aware of what's happening." It was a marked moment for me and I wrote it in my journal: "Something has happened."

My Mind Began to Open

I shared in previous chapters another episode that occurred shortly after this. My mom had asked me to look at the youth ministry to tell her what I could see, and I really didn't want to, but I went out of obedience.At this point in my healing I felt as though there was "cotton" in my brain. I just knew that there were parts of my soul that were not functioning. I was doing just the "basics" at that point. As I began to observe, it was as if something happened to my brain. It opened up, and I was fully aware of it! I saw clearly what needed to be done in that department. One of my jobs, prior to Marcus passing, was to assess departments and develop plans to make them better. That day in the Youth Ministry, I saw what I needed to see, and I knew something happened to my brain, that it opened up, and I knew God was saying to me, "Okay, you are healing Tracy, you are healing". There was still a long road ahead, but I knew something was happening.

I want to revisit the example of the dam. A lot of times we see pictures of a dam breaking. It looks colossal when all the water rushes in. It's as though it was a single event—that it just broke. The deal is that before the huge explosion, there are all these "little taps" that hit the wall and reduce the integrity of the dam. Tap. Tap. Tap. All those little taps are a part of a process that combine together and cause the water to burst through. I believe that every time I was just "showing up" in the presence of God, and I would say, "God, you Love Me," that anytime I spoke anything from His Word, there was a "tap" on my soul. All of those taps were starting to equal healing. Every time we go into the presence of God, whether we come corporately together or privately, it is an opportunity for God to impart life into us again. He is LIFE, a Life Force. So, if we are with Him, LIFE is coming on the inside of us.

I Began to Serve

Now, at six months my Pastor approached me to take on a new ministry department. It was a ministry department that I had never run. It was the Worship and Arts department. She wanted me to manage the music and also lead worship. Marcus not only taught the Bible at our church, but he also led all the Praise and Worship. He was extremely gifted. Prior to kids, I would back him up vocally, but I never led or organized Praise and Worship. Once we had children, I spent the majority of my time in Children's Ministry. I had never led worship in my life. I said, "Are you kidding me? What do I know about music?" She said, "Just do it, and trust God." I obeyed again! We had a small group doing the worship at that time, nothing like we have today. God just began to grow that thing, and I was just as shocked as everybody else, because I didn't know what I was doing. I would just show up, and God would give me what we needed to do. I'm the music director, and I don't even have a music degree! God has a sense of humor. I don't know how to read music. I knew nothing, and everybody was following me!? I thought that was such a joke, but God was in it. God was in it. The team grew. I remember the first time I had to lead worship I thought, "I don't know what I'm doing." I was shaking the whole time and thought "Let me teach please, but don't make me lead worship." God was with me. I was fully aware of His presence that would come on me for that task. People would say, "Wow, that was really great", and I was thinking, "You have no idea. I'm clueless." God, in His grace, equipped me for that task. We ended up having a choir and the thing just exploded (and I was just as shocked as everyone else). But this is what was interesting. My Pastor said, "I want you to do something." A lot of times when we go through something, a loss of some sort, we have a tendency to just kind of go "inward," "I just have to take care of me," and what we really need to do is focus outward and serve.

Purpose is a Great Antidote to a Suffering Heart

There is a season for only thinking of ourselves in allowing ourselves to heal, but it can't be too long. Something happened as I began to pour into this group of people. I couldn't pour music into them. What did I know about music? But, I was pouring the Word of God into them, into their families and basically loving on them. As I gave to that group of couples and families, on Sunday and Wednesday, God began to pour into me. Whatever we sow, we will reap. I was sowing seeds in an area that I needed to reap a harvest. So, I was sowing into "so and so's" marriage, and "so and so's" kid, and in this issue and that issue in our Worship and Arts department. I was sowing every Sunday leading worship, allowing God to just flow out of me. I was sowing and God just began to fill me. The healing escalated. As I began to serve others in spite of my own personal pain, God was healing me. The pain was still there, the loss was still there, but I purposed to serve and there was an escalation to the healing. I recognized that within a month of being in that department another change was happening.

It was much later when I understood why healing comes as we serve. We are made in the image of God. Our Father/Creator is a server. It's His nature. He is and always will be in a position to serve us. He is always out for us! Therefore, when we as humans step out and serve people, we are functioning in our original, created position. As we function in that position, harmony comes to the insides of our being.

There was such a grace on me! Everything I put my hand to in that season prospered. I really believe that God was saying, "You have every right to be at home and sulk, and have a pity party and all that, but you are giving." Purpose is a great antidote to a suffering heart. I had purpose working with that group. People's lives were being changed, and it was affecting me. My message to you is: get busy, don't just stay where you are. Find someone to help. Become part of a group. Begin to grow something, do something, and pour into something. Don't just think, "Oh, my Goodness, I have enough to do right now for me and my family. Look at this and look at that, we have enough to do." With that kind of thinking, we are limiting God. God is far bigger than our issues. God is far bigger than everything that we can see with our physical eye. He is inside of us, and wants to do tremendous things in us to help people, and to make a difference in the lives of the people that are in our communities.

By April, nine months later, I sensed I was stronger, but I still couldn't see color. Everything was just "blah." Did you ever have a cold, and you couldn't taste anything, and <u>everything</u> was just "blah"? That's what it was like for me, everything I saw was "blah."

My family was very strategic with my healing process. At strategic times they would say, "I think you need to go here, or do this." They planned this trip for me and the girls to go to Disney World Marcus' mother. We went, but I could really care less if I went. I could care less what we did, and I just remember that I was at Disney World, and I couldn't see color! Everything was a chore, I could care less about being there. I went along with it, the girls could use the distraction because there was still this healing process going on. I was aware that God was doing a mighty work in me, even though I still didn't see color. I knew that I was making progress in healing, so I kept showing up. I showed up, and stayed busy and cast down those wild imaginations (those thoughts that I wasn't getting anywhere, that I still had so much further to go). Layer by layer, bit by bit, God was healing my soul. I was thankful whenever an awareness of healing came, and focused on what healing I had received rather than focusing on what still needed to be accomplished. God is faithful. I knew that. I was receiving love. I positioned myself to receive God's love. I trusted Him to complete the healing He had started. It is a process. A process.

I continued to minister to others throughout the whole process. By August, things were really happening within our Worship and Arts department. We were growing and things were happening, God had indeed taken us to another level and I was feeling fulfilled and safe.

God Will Speak

At this particular time my Mom was encouraging me to think about remarriage and would often say, "Your kids need a father." I really didn't want to hear that. I can remember thinking, "Speak to the hand!" I told a close friend of mine, "I am so fulfilled in what I am doing. I'm married to Jesus." I was unaware that my mom felt she had heard from the Lord who my next husband was and that's why she was prodding me. I am so glad she didn't tell me. I wasn't ready, and I would have rebelled. My mom was extremely wise in how she handled me. My world was safe and manageable, I had my kids, Jesus was so real to me: I was happy.

In the month of August, one year after Marcus had passed, a man came to our church, who operated in a gift called the Gift of Prophecy. In the book of 1st Corinthians 12:9, the nine gifts of the Spirit are described. These spiritual gifts are when the Spirit of God comes on somebody and uses them in a supernatural way to speak things that have happened or are coming. This is what He spoke over me that day:

"I'm so pleased with you, the Lord says. My heart swells toward you. No, no, not 'cause you're tough, though sometimes you sure put on that thing, that garment of tough. No, no, not 'cause you're just kind of happy go lucky, no – even though sometimes people say, 'Isn't she happy

and full of joy and what's she's been through.' No, no, no, no, I'm pleased with you because you talk to Me. I'm pleased with you because you walk with Me, I'm pleased with you because you did not choose to turn to another. You did not choose to turn away, you've decided to stay tucked under My wing – ha, ha, ha. And that's what makes Me happy about you. And just like we're walking together now—the Lord says, you and Him, we're going to walk together and talk together in the days ahead, but know this: you do not have permission to marry Me for I have another. It is not My will that you walk like this, only for now, only for now, only for now. But great fulfillment in anointing, great fulfillment in blessing, great fulfillment in the ministry, and great fulfillment and satisfaction in your personal life. And now, you look forward and say, "I don't know, Lord," but then you'll look back and say, "Only the Lord My God could have done this for me, and made me so happy."

How did that man know that? He didn't know me from Adam. He basically said what I was doing every single day in my prayer chamber. As he was delivering this message from God, he kept walking with me on the stage. I was so heavily moved to tears because one of the things I said every single day was, "Lord, I am walking with You." I would walk around in my house as if God were walking next to me. I'd say, "Lord, I'm walking with you, just like Adam walked with you in the cool of the day, I'm walking with you, God, I'm not alone you are with me." No one knew I did that! But God spoke through him. That was one year after Marcus passed. Another interesting point is that the week prior to this man coming to our church I said, "I'm married to Jesus!" God is merciful and so compassionate. My mom, I'm pretty sure was saying, "It's about time!" The Lord comforted my Mom by telling her that within two years I would be settled. She kept all that from me. She knew I was so tied to Marcus, I didn't want to hear anything. Notice in the prophecy he said, "You didn't turn to another, you stayed close to Me." I simply showed up in His presence. I wasn't sure I always knew what to say, or do, but I showed up and He honored me.

Questions for Chapter 17:

1. Purpose is an antidote to a _____ _____.

2. What can escalate healing?

3. As we step out to serve people, we are functioning in our _____ _____ position.

Reflect:

Have you felt as if you only had enough energy for the day to supply yourself? Have you wanted to isolate yourself? If we feed those feelings we are going in the opposite direction of healing.

Act:

Whether or not you feel like it, find someone to serve, someone to give to. Trust God that as you are giving to others, God is perfecting the things that concern you.

Study question answers found on pages 184-190

Chapter 18: See a Future

It was hard to believe that God had a vision and a purpose for my life in the midst of the tragedy. I had to, on purpose, look frequently at the promise of a great future and a hope written about in Jeremiah 29:11. Martha Munizzi wrote a song about that Scripture called, "I Know the Plans I Have for You." I would sing that song over and over during the healing process. I didn't "feel" like there was a plan for my life. Have you ever been there, where you don't feel like there's a plan for your life, when you don't feel like there's purpose or vision for you? It's a big lie! Every person created in the image of God, who has Christ on the inside of them, has a purpose and a vision—something that they are supposed to do to make a difference while they are on this earth. We have to accept that God has a vision for our lives. Even in the midst of tragedy, He has a vision of our glorious future. No matter what has happened in my life, the good or the bad, I have had to believe that God has a vision for me, and it's a plan to prosper me and to give me a future and a hope.

We Have to Let Go of the Past

In order to go forward with that vision, we have to let go of the past. In Philippians 3:13, the Apostle Paul admonishes us to "forget what is behind and strain toward what is ahead."

There is a tendency, when we've gone through tragedies,

when we've gone through loss, for us to look backwards more than look ahead. We have a hard time looking ahead, <u>because</u> we still want what was; that person, that marriage, or that dream. We want to return to what we know, what we understand, and what we wanted. God says, "No, you need to let that go, and on purpose turn your face toward your future." Even regarding mistakes, we have to let go. We replay our mistakes in our minds over and over which serves only to keep us in the past. God is not in that! He wants us to go forward. He is not rehearsing our mistakes. He is not looking back.We can't allow our past to hold back our future. We have to let go of that past to go forward. God is a creator. He wants to create something new in us. There is nothing new in the past, there is only something new in the future, so we need to stay out of the past, and partner with God and watch Him create and shape a glorious future.

Our Words Shape our Future

The words that come out of our mouths play a huge part in shaping our future. I talked about this quite a bit in chapter 11. However I want to revisit a few things. In Romans 4:17, the Apostle Paul gives clues to the workings of God when he said:

As it is written: "I have made you a father of many nations." He is our father in the sight of God, in whom he believed—the God who gives life to the dead and calls things that are not as though they were.

This Scripture is referring to the time when God called Abraham a "Father of many nations" long before he ever had one child! Abraham, in the course of time, believed the impossible. He believed that in his old age he could conceive. When the Scripture above says, "the God who gives life to the dead..." Abraham and Sarah's bodies were both dead regarding their ability to have children (especially in their old age; she was 90 and he was 99), but God "calls things that are not as though they were." I mentioned in chapter 11 that when Abraham began to call himself what God was calling him, something miraculous happened. It took three months of calling himself "a father of many" and Sarah "a mother of many" that caused their bodies to miraculously line up and birth a baby! God told Abraham way before He ever had his first child that out of Abraham's seed all the nations of the earth would be blessed. God was referring to the Christ, Who came out of the lineage of Abraham!

The point is this: God calls things to be before they are! From God's perspective, it was done. Abraham was the father, so agreeing with His word brought God's reality in to this earthly realm. When our words line up with what God says about our lives, miraculous things can happen! Our words are creative in origin, because we are made in the image of God Who creates things with words.

I also mentioned in that same chapter how science and doctors are proving the power of the spoken word. Many times we do this with our kids. We begin to see a certain gifting and start to say what we think they are going to do. My daughter, at a young age, had a gifting with music. I knew she could and would lead worship one day. I would say to her often, "You're going to lead worship." She has begun to do so now!

We Have to Cooperate with God's Good Plan for Our Lives

We can shape our future! I knew these principles and so when that prophet came and prophesied over my life that God had someone for me, I knew I had to cooperate with it. More so, my mother did! Right after the prophecy came (mentioned in Chapter 17), my mom looked at me and asked, "So what do you plan to do with this prophecy?" I can remember thinking, "I'm going to stand on the corner shouting, 'Hey I'm single, are you interested?'" I was being very sarcastic.

I remembered reading about the power of our words from **The Fourth Dimension** by Paul Yonggi Cho, where a woman desired to get married, but it wasn't happening. She was in her thirties and was a little concerned, so she went to Dr. Cho, asking him to pray for her. Before he prayed for her, he asked her what she wanted in a man and she began to describe what she desired. Dr. Cho was doing this because he believed she needed to be specific and get a clear-cut picture of what she wanted. When she had that clear picture, he then prayed for her. She continued to keep that picture before her by speaking out that specific picture she had. Several months later a young man came to her church that fit the description to the tee, however all the young girls in the church were constantly surrounding him. This young man, however, was drawn to the older woman and within a year they were married.[1]

If God brought that story to my remembrance then obviously He was requiring of me to do something, to make my requests and get specific as well! It took me a while to get a clear-cut picture. I finally wrote down precisely what I thought I would need. I wrote down three specific as well!

It took me a while to get a clear-cut picture. I finally wrote down precisely what I thought I would need. I wrote down three specific areas: spiritual, soulful and physical attributes. There were about 15 qualities. I was very specific. I can remember looking at my list and thinking this will take a miracle, if God pull this off, I will definitely marry!

I got as far as making the list, but I wasn't really consistent in keeping that clear picture before me, praying and declaring those things I wrote. (We need to remember Abraham, he consistently heard himself say "Father of many" for three months and then he saw it in his life.)

God Ratted Me Out

I still don't know why I didn't take it seriously, but my mom did. One day, while she was walking, she was asking God when He was going to bring someone into my life. She asked, "When is the man coming? Why hasn't it happened?" God spoke to her, "It's your daughter's fault. She's not speaking about it to Me. She is not calling it to be as she knows to do." Can you believe that? God ratted me out to my mom!

My mother had an understanding that the girls were young enough to gravitate toward someone new if a father figure would soon enter into their lives. She strongly desired the girls to have the opportunity to grow with such a father figure, which is so commendable, and I appreciated it. My mom promptly called me over to her house. I had no idea I was about to experience the wrath of Mom! As soon as I walked into her house she said,

"You're not speaking your list. You're not even going to God with that list are you?" I said, "I am...a little." She said, "Tracy, God wants to do something in your life, and you know better. He wants to cooperate with you. You know how to do this!"

For most of the things that I've received from God, I've had to search the Word to find Scriptures that addressed my particular situation that needed to change. In a sense, I had to "build a case" on the inside of me so that I had an understanding of what God's will was for me in that area. What happens is, the Word would get in me so much that I would believe what God said over what I saw, and then the manifestation would soon come. I had to know, that I know, that I know that God wanted me to walk in wholeness and freedom.

I didn't have quick-answered prayers. I usually had to put the principles that I had been taught to practice. But that's why my faith grew, that's how my faith grew, because I had to learn how to exercise it. It is like muscles in the natural. If I want my biceps to grow bigger, stronger and leaner, I have to exercise them. After consistent, dedicated work, I always saw results. It is the same with faith. We pick it up and put it into practice, and we will see it work.

I knew then how vital it was for me to cooperate fully with God. God truly knew what was best for me and the girls, and He was waiting on me. Imagine that, He was waiting on me. This is a big revelation that God, many times, is waiting on us to perform the things we desire! If we are not seeing a manifestation of prayer, let's not lump all the reasons into "it's not my time yet". Maybe we need to cooperate more. I thank God that I know what I know, and that you do too, so we can get busy doing our part, so that God can fulfill His agreement. From that day forward I faithfully prayed "the list" and got that clear-cut picture.

Something Began to Happen...

After about three months of saying those specific qualities and standing on specific promises from God, something began to happen on the inside of me. I no longer saw myself single. It's really strange, but I saw myself as "spoken for." I remember being in a service where a gentleman wanted all the single women to stand so he could pray for them. I should have stood. However, inside of me something was different. On the inside, I wasn't single. On the inside, my understanding was fully that I was married. Faith sees things done, things that "be not," before the eye sees in the natural.

Shortly thereafter, I had a mini vision of a young man lying on his side. I didn't see his face, only his curly hair. I knew from the vision that he was my future husband. The funny thing about the vision was the hair. I remember thinking, "I don't like curly hair on men." I had put hair color on my list, but not the kind of hair!

In this same time period a gentleman came to me at a church service telling me a strange dream he had about me. In the dream he said that I was in some store shopping and he could see me through a window. He saw me putting a mannequin together, and in the process I would place the certain body parts in place, step back and assess. He said, "It was so strange, Tracy. You would place the head, then you would step back and take a good look, then you would put the arms in place. If you didn't like it, you would take it off and try something else. All I knew is that you were shaping a man of some sort." He was bewildered by the dream. I wasn't. I knew the dream was to show me that my words were shaping my future, that my words were doing something! I was so shocked by the dream and the humorous mercy of God and His awesome love for me.

Obedience is a Profound Key

Something strange happened in January 2004. I was walking through the house, and I had this impression that I was supposed to start working out. I totally dismissed it at first because I weighed only 102 pounds. Throughout the whole month I kept sensing this, yet kept dismissing it. Finally I asked my mom about it and she said, "You'd better obey God and start working out." I was so shocked that she said this! Working out means time and I did not have time. Mom was always big about how I used my time. I thought for sure she was going to say, "God would not tell you to work out. It must be the pizza you ate last night." My mother did not let on that she already knew who my new husband was, and she knew how extremely important working out was to him. Mom had some inside information.

My mom lives very close to me and about a month prior to this she was walking outside and was about to stop by. Upon approaching my house she was talking to God about who I was supposed to marry.

She actually was talking to God about a particular man that she knew was interested in me. God spoke to her and said, "He is not for her. Tracy needs someone young for her children." As soon as she heard God speak, she came around the corner of my house to find James, who is now my husband, playing with my kids on our playset in our yard. She knew in her heart, "That's Tracy's husband."

James is my brother's brother-in-law (James' sister is married to my brother). My brother and sister-in-law live next door to me, so James was frequently around visiting his sister and nieces (my brother has three girls as well). I had known James for twelve years. He had been a part of our church prior to moving out of state for his job. He'd been away from Michigan for five years. Upon moving back to Michigan, he purchased a condo one mile from my house. Being the bachelor that he was, he would show up where the food was, which was either my house or his sister's! It was very easy for James to be around our family.

In sheer obedience to what I felt God telling me to do, I began to work out and to run. I did not enjoy it at all! In this time period, James seemed to be coming around our family more and more. Unfortunately, I viewed James as very shallow and in dire need of help. I did not understand him. Have you ever judged someone by the cover? He respected my counsel and opinion and therefore would frequently run things by me. He would often sit on my counter and allow me to dissect why he was making the choices that he made.

In one of our "counter times" we were discussing relationships. He had been in a three-year relationship which had ended. I knew he had to care deeply for that woman to stay that long in a relationship. I was actually trying to encourage him to consider going back to her. He had mentioned that she was beautiful, extremely smart, fun, and adventurous. She seemed to enjoy all the things that James enjoyed. I finally asked, "What is your problem? She sounds incredible!" He hesitated, then said, "She is incredible. I just don't think she'll be a great mom." I was stunned! I considered him shallow, but this response was far from shallow! It got my attention. I had a new respect for him and realized I had boxed him in! His sister and I began to play matchmaker, wondering who we could introduce him to. As those introductions were being made, we still continued in our friendship. He helped me with fitness and I helped him with life!

My Healing Complete

In April 2004, my whole family (my children, brothers, sisters-in-law, nieces and nephews) took a vacation to Disney World. I had just been there less than a year before, but my brothers had never been there with their children, so we packed up and went. It was on this trip that the Lord spoke clearly to me that my healing was complete. I mentioned in the beginning of this book how my family knew it as well. I had a new zest for life.

After returning from our vacation I hurt my hip running. I was told by my sports medicine physician that I should only be biking until my hip healed. James was an avid biker, specifically mountain biking, and therefore took it upon himself to help me learn the ropes of mountain biking. He was adamant about coming with me to buy all my gear. Once all my stuff was purchased, he took me on my first ride. Our first ride was so difficult for me. I seriously almost threw up! I was determined to overcome the hills! Every opportunity we had, we hit the trails. In the middle of all this, he began working in our TV department at church, which was an area I was overseeing as well. It seemed that he began to show up in so many areas of my life, which allowed me to see his character. More and more I would stop and think, "I like that about his character." He seemed to be everywhere I was; family events, church events, our community pool.

This is what I find very humorous. While all this was going on, my brother and sister-in-law were setting me up with various men. I would say yes about a meeting, but would always cancel at the last minute. I just wasn't interested.

The Mercy of God in Knowing Me

As I look back, I recognize the mercy of God. God knew that I had walls up regarding relationships. James, however, was not an option in my mind for a relationship, and so I was open. I could be myself, and I was not threatened at all by him. When I was with James I allowed myself to have a blast. I can remember thinking, "Wow, I can have fun with a guy and not be afraid he'll fall for me or I'll fall for him." What is so funny is that he felt the same way! He didn't want to fall into a relationship again. He wanted to grow in his identity as a Christian and I was safe to hang out with because, in his mind, I would never engage in a romantic relationship with him. Neither of us tried to impress or win the other person, we simply enjoyed our recreation and companionship. We were both there for each other when we needed someone to talk to, someone to email at the end of our day, someone we felt safe and comfortable around. I remember one email James sent me where he wrote something regarding finding him a woman who was just like me. I responded, "Impossible, God broke the mold when He made me." I was so fresh! (I'm so glad

I saved several of the emails he sent me!)

My mom has often said, "If you put two matches together, they are going to light." Family and friends around us began to notice how we would gravitate toward each other in all environments. Still, in my brain, he was not an option. One day, a friend of mine called confronting me regarding James. She said, "Are you blind! Can't you see the way he looks at you? James has it for you." I laughed, however it made me think. I took an honest look and realized I really did enjoy his company and I really looked forward to seeing him. I looked for his emails.

After that phone call from my friend I think I became more sensitive, more open, and more aware. Finally, after seeing James every day for three weeks straight, I asked, "Is there something going on with us?" He answered, "Well, yeah!" We both began to express our care for each other and in the same breath our caution. We decided that day that we were going to go through a season to see if we truly were compatible for each other as well as presenting to both family and the pastoral staff at Life Christian Church their opinions of our being together. To our amazement family and pastors were already in agreement.

James and I began to devour books that would cause us to take an honest look at our relationship. The first book we read was called **Home Improvement** by Bishop Keith Butler.2 It opened up plenty of discussion. We went through pre-marital counseling as well. Again, to our amazement, we were extremely compatible. We shared the same beliefs regarding God, family, finances, raising children, sex and extended family. I was shocked at how James was fitting my extremely specific list I had made!

By August 2004, James and I both knew we were for each other. It was exactly two years! (Remember the Lord spoke to my mom that I would be settled in two years?) Even though I knew we were to be together I still took it slowly. I wanted the girls to welcome James on their own, not because they had too. My greatest concern was my oldest daughter. She had a hard time with Marcus' passing because she was old enough to understand and remember him. I was truly waiting to see her be completely settled about my moving on.

One morning my oldest daughter came to me to tell me a dream she had. In the dream her father came to her letting her know that he was so happy that James was in my life and that he wanted her to be happy as well. He continued to tell her he was happy she would have a father. After she told me the dream she said, "Mom, it's okay to marry James." She had no idea I was waiting.

Shortly after that, James took my girls out for dinner and asked them if he could marry me. They all agreed! In January of 2005 James proposed to me, with the girls present, placing a ring on my finger as well as all the girls' fingers! In May of 2005, we were married.

Boyd Fam

The Wedding Ceremony Uniting
Tracy Stefano
And
James Boyd

Sunday, May 1, 2005
Life Christian Church
Troy, Michigan

End notes:
1.   Paul Yongii Cho-. Fourth Dimension-Pages18-21, South Plainfield, AL: Bridge Publishing, Inc, 1979.
2.   Butler, Bishop Keith & Debra. Home Improvement. Southfield: Word of Faith Publishing, 2001.

Questions for Chapter 18:
1.   In order to go forward with our future we have to___
_____.

2.   What molds our lives?

3.   According Romans 4:17, what did Abraham have to do to receive God's promise?

4.   What is a "profound key to obtaining God's will?"

Reflect:
Have you had a hard time letting go of the past? Maybe you are rehearsing the "what ifs?" Is that kind of thinking helping you or holding you back? Are you ready to go forward? If you are then say, "According to Philippians 3:13, I choose to let go of the past and strain toward what is ahead."

Act:
Begin to write down some things that you want to see in your future. Work on this until you have a clear picture in your mind. Make sure to involve God, talking to Him throughout the process.

Study question answers found on pages 184-190

Live Again

A true story of overcoming los

Chapter 19: Conclusion

It's been several years since Marcus' passing. I am still amazed at the awesome grace by which God walked me through the healing process. It was, and will probably always be, the most difficult heart-wrenching time of my life. The greatest understanding that has come out of all of this for me is that no matter what I face, God has a way of escape and is able to take me to the other side unscathed!

Although I have experienced tremendous healing and I am very fulfilled personally, it is still hard whenever I have to talk again to my girls when they are struggling. I hate to see them struggle! It seems almost every year they ask questions again regarding the whole event. I have learned that I must pray for their complete process of healing. Because they were young when the passing happened, we revisit the "why" as well as certain healing aspects yearly.

One of my girls had a harder time than the others because she was older when Marcus died, therefore she had a greater understanding of what was truly happening. She experienced feelings of abandonment, rejection and great insecurity. Recently, I recognized that she was unwilling to let go of the pain she had experienced in his loss for fear she would somehow forget him, thinking that if she let go of the pain, she was letting go of him. I had to walk her through this, letting her know that is not what he would want of her. He would want her to remember him for who he was and accepting a new future was okay.

It is so important for us to receive healing for ourselves so we can give it to our children. When you are healing from loss, it is not the time to get involved with someone new unless you and your children have been going through a healing process together. I was completely accountable to pastors and family members in my life, as well as my children, when the courting season began with James. They would have advised me to wait if they saw I still needed time to heal, and I would have trusted that they had my best interest in mind, whether I understood it or not. I'm so grateful for my family. They helped me stand on the Word when my body was weak, they were my voices of reason and kept me protected so I could heal completely.

It is necessary to heal so that we do not take baggage into the next relationship.

I heard people say, "You can never be healed of a loss. No one could ever fill that place." There's some truth regarding the filling. Nobody will be exactly the same or possess the same characteristics. In my experience, however, God healed me in such a way that when I think of that season of my life it's as if it had happened to another person. That hole that Marcus' loss left, isn't there anymore. It didn't get filled with his replica, but what was once a gaping hole is now gone. It's as if I didn't walk through it. It's as though someone else walked through it for me. God is so supernatural that He has a way of going into the very soul of a man and doing a work that no man can see. He does a work that no counselor can do, that no vocation can do. He does a work that is so full of love that allows you to look at the most devastating situation and say, "Oh my God, that happened to me?" It is amazing when you have walked with God through a situation that the world would tell you could only destroy you, and you look back, and you can't even understand that it did, in fact, happen to you.

When you look at it with your natural eyes, even you don't understand how you survived, let alone came out victorious. Because you walked through it in God's strength, because God enabled each step you took and because God gave you the grace you needed for each moment of each day—because He did all the work, you are unaware of how much He truly has you covered at the time. Then, you look back at it and don't understand how you made it through. That's the God who I walked with. I'm eternally grateful for that. Without His healing, I couldn't have gone forward.

My healing didn't happen overnight. It was a process. I have learned to be okay with my process, and you will too. I looked to God, purposed to be surrounded by an environment that promoted healing with the Word of God, His Holy Spirit, the Love of God and the Body of Christ. I consistently exercised the authority, in the Name of Jesus, given to me as a believer whether I had the strength to do it on my own, or had others to help me. It was not always easy. It was not always natural to my mind and body. Sometimes it was ugly. At other times not as ugly, but it was still a fight.

From beginning to end, it was an eighteen-month process. My spiritual father, Bishop Butler told me it was going to take about two years to heal.

I will tell you that I knew, and so did those close to me know, when it was over. I want to encourage you, that no matter where you are in your healing process, whether you experienced loss years ago, or just today, that through joining with God and finding the hope, strength and power available in His Word, your soul will receive complete healing that only He is able to provide. I want to encourage you that you too, will someday, in the not so-distant-future know the exact time that your healing is complete, and you, too, will Live Again.

Live Again

A true story of overcoming loss

Study Questions

Answers to Chapter 3 Questions:

1. Because Adam disobeyed God and listened to the devil's voice, sin was ushered into the earth, causing negative things to press against anything that is good.

2. Our spirit. We become children of God with the potential to navigate through a negative world and still be victorious.

3. When the devil hurts humanity, he hurts God.

Answers to Chapter 4 Questions:

1. Our environments: observations, associations and teachings.

2. Yes.

3. Envy, bitterness, un-forgiveness, anything negative.

Answers to Chapter 5 Questions:

1. Tragedies, storms, trials are a result of a fallen world that is flawed—where negativity is pressing against anything that is good: choices that we've made, choices of those who love us or those who are in our lives have made, and demonic influences.

2. Healing from God...He is the only One who can heal our soul.

Answers to Chapter 6 Questions:

1. It can lead to depression and feelings of no longer wanting to live.

2. Pain

3. Yes

Answers to Chapter 7 Questions:

1. Holy Spirit.

2. Joy and eternal pleasures.

3. We will run and not grow weary; we will walk and not faint.

4. The negative stuff for His healing stuff.

Answers to Chapter 8 Questions:

1. Heal, preserve, save, and do well

2. Medicine

Answers to Chapter 9 Questions:

1. Receiving the Love of God

2. Something

3. By simply saying, "God, You love me. I receive your love."

Answers to Chapter 10 Questions:

1. Encourage

2. Yes. It plays a large part in shaping who we are.

Answers to Chapter 11 Questions:

1. It is our nature to say what our senses say versus what God says or the solution that we are seeking says.

2. 3 months

Answers to Chapter 12 Questions:

1. Adam and Eve. When they listened and followed Satan's voice instead of God's

2. By using our authority in Christ once we receive Him in our hearts.

3. The Word of God

4. The Name of Jesus Christ

Answers to Chapter 13 Questions

1. Destructive thoughts/imaginations

2. The Word of God

3. Positive, negative

Answers to Chapter 14 Questions:

1. Unmerited favor, moral strength or the divine assistance to perform a duty, a divine influence upon the heart

2. We receive it.

3. Focus on the good.

4. Think on things that are true, noble, right, pure, lovely, admirable.

Answers for Chapter 15 Questions:

1. Dreams

2. The Word of God

3. Pain

Answers to Chapter 16 Questions:

1. Powerful to do something, bring change

2. Healing, thought

3. Because they live in a fallen world.

4. We are.

Answers to Chapter 17 Questions:

1. Suffering heart

2. Healing

3. Original, created

Answer to Chapter 18 Questions

1. Let go of the past

2. Words

3. Call things to be before they are

4. Obedience

Live Again

A true story of overcoming los

Bibliography

Yongii Cho, Paul. Fourth Dimension. South Plainfield, AL: Bridge Publishing, Inc, 1979.

Leaf, Caroline. Who Switched Off My Brain. Switch off your Brain PTY Ltd, 2007.

Cherry, Reginald. The Bible Cure. Orlando: Creation House, 1998.

Other books by this author:

This book is intended to answer all of your questions regarding the Holy Spirit in your life. This is a must read for those who desire to go another level in their walk with Christ as it pertains to walking with the Holy Spirit.

This book describes your first steps after becoming a follower of Christ. Many people who have read this book, have defined it as the most effective resource that they have come across to really give a full understanding of what they received when they were saved and steps to grow closer to Christ.